heart and his pen." –**James M. Wilson, Chair, Department of English, Flagler College, Retired**

"In Thom Brucie's novel, *Obsidian Mirth*, Daniel Reed's wife develops adult-onset schizophrenia. Daniel's personal perspective of this experience allows the reader to enter into the bewilderment of mental illness within a family, especially the difficult tensions between forgiveness and healing. It is a powerful story, and this book is going to help families not just to cope but also to heal." –**H. K. Morey, LCSW, Licensed Clinical Social Worker**

Obsidian Mirth

Thom Brucie

En Route Books and Media, LLC

Saint Louis, MO

⊕ENROUTE
Make the time

En Route Books and Media, LLC
5705 Rhodes Avenue
St. Louis, MO 63109

Cover credit: Sebastian Mahfood

Author photo copyright Carol Brucie
Editorial Suggestions: Theresa Winchell

ISBN-13: 978-1-956715-45-3
Library of Congress Control Number
2022936313

Unless you utter by the tongue
words easy to understand,
how will be known
what is spoken?

1 Corinthians 13: 9

Chapter 1

A man must love unconditionally. No bartering with guilt, such as: I said I love you; now you say you love me. No quid pro quo, such as: if we have sex tonight, I will buy that necklace you want. Love is not a bargaining chip. It is an attitude that proclaims in actions the words I love you without conditions, in spite of disagreements, with never an effort to change her, while continuing to love her as she changes.

Love is not 50/50, 60/40, or 80/20. It is not even 100/100. Love is 100/0. When a man loves, he gives everything he's got, and he expects nothing in return. He loves unequivocally because he loves. Love is love. That's it. And when a man loves a woman, he loves her. One hundred percent. Nothing less. Anything less is not love. It's something else. It could be almost love; or maybe great like; or even something such as admiration. But real love is real love. It's all the way. It's indomitable. It's life-long.

And –

And, love binds with a delicate strand. Any man who truly loves a woman can hope she loves him in return, but he cannot require it, and it doesn't always work out that way, and when it doesn't, then what?

Chapter 2

I found a newborn field mouse, fallen from its nest, on the floor of the storage pantry behind our kitchen. I was about ten years old. I cupped the little thing in my hand.

"There you go," I said and dropped him back into the nest of chewed paper and frayed rags.

Almost immediately the little mouse worked his way over the top of the nest again and slid to a soundless, sudden stop as it hit the floor. He lifted his nose into the air, jerking his head from side to side with the inquisitive, uncoordinated muscles of the very young.

"What happened?" I asked. "You're a real explorer, aren't you?"

I returned the almost weightless bundle to its nest. I put a bag of potatoes in front of the box to create a barrier. I found something else to do, it being summer and all, but the next morning I discovered the little mouse in the pantry with its hind legs and tail sticking out of our tomcat's guilty mouth.

"That's what you get when you interfere in another's life," Doctor Leonard admonished. "By helping in one arena you leave that creature open to a different danger, one perhaps it is even less able to manage."

"Is that true with people too?" I asked.

"Of course," he said. "Almost always. But the point is, Daniel . . ." He paused a moment to draw on his pipe. A small cloud of smoke arose from the side of his mouth.

"The point is, that's a flaw you have, needing to fix things for everybody. What you call helping is really enabling."

He puffed on his pipe again, discharging smoky exhalations that animated his professional advice.

"You should learn to put yourself first. Then," he concluded, "other people's problems, Charlene's problems, won't bother you so much."

I knew he was trying to help me, but I thought that if I had it to do over, I would put the little mouse back in the nest again. A similar sort of accident happened the night I met Charlene, and in spite of the consequences, I would do it over again, too.

I met her the first semester of my sophomore year at Marysville College.

I had to work my way through school, and the owner of The Bistro Du Vin, Ronaldo Geordano, gave me a job as a dishwasher. I worked for him for three years at The Bistro, and later, he helped me get started in business.

The Bistro was a yuppie eatery with live music on the weekends and a bar that carried local California wine labels. The interior decorator that Ronaldo hired stained the plaster walls pale chartreuse and hung expensive original prints by up-and-coming artists from San Francisco. Each table had four dark maroon captain's chairs, and Ronaldo made an event of it when a group of six or more called in and he squared up two tables to accommodate them. He made friends with a nearby florist, and each table had fresh flowers every week. In addition, the florist sent along a large display vase that Ronaldo placed on an old, oak wine cask at the entrance.

That display, and Ronaldo's affection toward it, got me and Charlene into some trouble.

It happened the first night I saw her.

Ronaldo hired her as a waitress, and when I looked out through the passage window in the kitchen, I beheld an aura of light around her as if the sun sent down a second cousin to keep her company. She seemed tall, with statuesque legs. The uniform fit her so well you'd have thought Ronaldo designed it for her; short black skirt, black heels, and the fitted black vest pulled tightly around a fluffy white blouse. Ronaldo wanted the girls to look like the high priced liquor waitresses at Reno and most of them did. Charlene looked like a waitress princess.

She had white skin, so white I figured she must be from back east where it snows, Ohio, or Michigan, or someplace like that. Not just white, though, flawless. Skin with no blemishes and no wrinkles. And the red lipstick Ronaldo required the waitresses to wear made her lips so sensual against that white skin that I wanted to kiss her. Her black hair fell to just above the shoulders, and when she walked, her hair bounced with a nonchalance that made her look brazen and confident.

In an instant I loved her. Well, sort of love. Love at first sight kind of thing. Enough of an emotion that I wanted to meet her.

Here in California, love grows not in the delicate language of poets. No. Here love flourishes in audacious sensationalism. In other words, to win the girl, you must show your feathers. So, peacock bright, I decided to impress her with the boldest choice available to me, a flower from Ronaldo's special display at the entrance. That night, the arrangement contained scarlet fuchsia, delicate pink laurel, yellow poppies, and white calla lilies.

I walked past the shiny walnut reservation lectern to the hand-thrown, red clay vase resting on the old wine cask. I chose a luscious, erotic lily from the center of the display, its green stem trickling water like sweat. I lifted the opulent white flower to my nose to smell it, and it had no smell, a compliment to the science of hot-house horticulture.

I walked around the corner, and luckily Charlene stood alone at the waitress station, writing in her order book. I walked up to her.

"Hi," I said.

"Hi," she replied.

She looked right at me, direct, clear-eyed, as if no one had ever described for her the strategy of coyness in mating negotiations. It startled me into silence, so we stood, facing one another, in an awkward and unblinking stillness.

Finally, I said, "I'm Daniel," and lifted my arm and

stretched the pointed, white tip of the lily toward her.

She didn't move.

"It's for you," I said.

I jiggled the lily and pushed it toward her again.

She took the stalk and smiled.

"Thank you," she said. "It's nice."

She set the flower on a nearby shelf and returned to her work at the order desk.

I began to feel alone, and with a suddenness born of awkwardness, the noise of the restaurant returned, clanging dishes and the congested words of blended conversations.

"Nice meeting you," I said as I hurried to return to the dishwasher. She hadn't told me her name, but I think she smiled when my back was turned.

Normally, the bus-boys stacked the dishes on the table, threw the silverware in a flat tray, and placed the glasses in a glass tray. They pulled the paper, straws, and trash, and they put the dirty linen in the laundry bin. It was a good system that helped me keep ahead of any demand for clean tableware. I did pots, pans, and fryers after we closed.

A couple of dish trays had backed up, and Ronaldo displayed some consternation by standing near the door and flailing his hand, first at me, then at the dirty dishes, and then at me again.

I smiled at him and sang, "Some enchanted evening, you may see a stranger," and I danced across the wooden floor grids to the other side of the dishwasher. Ronaldo waved a semi-cupped hand in exasperation like a conductor ending a Sousa march.

"Da dadaa da dada," I hummed and pushed the first tray into the washer until the bottom caught on the pulley chain. Then the second. And then I took the rinsing hose and sprayed the wash table and the dishes which hadn't been trayed yet, and then I sprayed the wall and the wooden walk, and then I stopped when I realized that not only Ronaldo, but also the chef, the cooks, and two of the waitresses stopped work to watch me. I raised my eyebrows and grinned, let the hose snap back into place, and headed to the other end of the dishwasher as the first tray emerged, my impromptu opus at an end.

It was a good night, for me and for Ronaldo. I gave a flower to a beautiful woman. Ronaldo turned all twenty tables, and the bar crowd was drinking.

Ronaldo came to the back.

"Feeling spunky tonight, eh?"

"Hey, Ronaldo."

I pulled a tray of dishes and placed it on the dry rack. Ronaldo nodded as he inspected my work. He never said much about it for two reasons. First, usually I did pretty good work, and second, he couldn't stand getting his clothes soiled, so he never moved too close to messy areas. I reached to pull a flat tray of silverware from the stack on the prep table.

Simultaneously, Ronaldo and I said, "What's that?"

Lying on top of the silverware, we saw the withered remains of the calla lily. The stem had lost its moisture and looked wrinkled and shriveled. The flower looked like a drowned potato skin, decrepit and limp.

"What is that?" Ronaldo demanded again.

"Well, it's . . ."

"Who put that there?"

"I guess the new girl. She had it."

I felt stung. Wounded. Was this a message from her? How could she treat my gift that way? It had to be a mistake, but love, I'm sure, generally misses the oblique, and I should have seen it as an omen.

Ronaldo wasn't thinking about romance. Someone had stolen from him, taken a flower from his entrance arrangement.

Finally, I gathered myself and turned to explain things, but Ronaldo had already left.

He went directly to Charlene and fired her.

Chapter 3

Naturally, I did not know that Ronaldo fired Charlene until the next night when she didn't show up at The Bistro. The waitresses seemed grumpy working shorthanded, but Ronaldo ignored their complaints. I didn't ask about her because I thought she was upset with me. Maybe my flirtation had been too audacious. When I did learn about her firing, I felt responsible, and left to my own talents, I might never have gotten her job back. Fortunately, my friend Mark intervened.

Mark and I shot pool two or three times a month at Johnny's Billiards. I met him there after work. When I arrived, Mark was finishing a rack.

"No matter how much you practice, you can't beat me," I told him.

He didn't say anything. Instead, he pointed the tip of his cue stick at a nearby table. On it sat two bottles of beer and an ashtray. One of the bottles was half empty. I took the full one and sat down. A cigarette leaned from Mark's mouth. His long arms stroked the cue seven or eight times, searching for the perfect spot. He tilted his head to allow a stream of smoke to curl past his cheek and around his eyes, and finally he struck the ball.

"Damn," he said as the eight ball touched the lip of the side pocket and rolled up the rail. He walked to the table, and picked up his beer. We touched bottles and took a long swallow.

"Rack 'em," he said.

I pulled the balls from the leather pockets and set the rack. I rolled the cue ball to the far end of the table and went to pick out a cue. Johnny kept a good supply of sticks, and he kept them clean with fresh tips. I chose an eighteen ouncer.

Mark waited to lag for the break

"Go ahead," I said.

He tapped the cue ball. It hit the cushion and rolled back to about three inches from the rail.

"Good enough," I said, and conceded the break. I needed a minute to rough up the cue tip.

Mark liked to break off the side of the second ball in the rack because he could sink the eight ball if he hit it just right. Sometimes it worked. We played that if you sink the eight on the break, you win the game. Mark liked to do that, because otherwise I killed him. We might play twenty games on a long night, and I'd win seventeen of them.

I used a dime to scratch the cue tip. Dimes work better than any other coin if you don't have sandpaper or a tip pic. I like to rough up all the way around the edge and then scuff the center to raise little frays of leather. That roughened surface catches the cue ball for better english. Something Johnny showed me.

As the ridges of the dime began to shard the outer edge of the tip, I heard the cue ball scatter the rack.

"Three ball. I've got solids."

I nodded.

Mark sank a second ball and a third one, but he missed the fourth. I'll give him this – once he broke, he didn't move the balls around with sloppy rolls. He made me earn my shots.

I tried for the thirteen in the side. "I met a girl at work," I said, and sank the ball with a little reverse to set up for the fifteen in the upper corner.

"What's her name?"

"I don't know."

"That's always a good way to meet someone."

I tapped the fifteen with a little top left and played the cue off the cushion to set up for the eleven.

"Funny," I said.

I knocked in the eleven harder than I should have, and the cue ball jumped off the table.

Mark watched it roll and twisted his lips into a smirk, but he made no effort to retrieve it.

"She was working at The Bistro, and it's my fault she got fired."

I walked past him to get the cue ball, ignoring Johnny's glare. He didn't like people to abuse his tables. I handed the ball to Mark.

"That explains everything," he said.

Yeah, I thought, and went to get two more beers. I put two dollars on the counter. Johnny slipped two beers between his fingers, lifted them out of the cooler, and set them before me.

"Sorry about that shot, Johnny," I said.

He accepted the two bills, tapped the edges on the counter, and pointed them at me. Forgiven, I nodded and returned to the game.

Mark stood at the far end of the table, looking about as patient as a school principal waiting for a student who cannot control his enjoyment of spitballs. He motioned with his head to the table. He was ready to shoot the eight ball. He touched the corner pocket with the tip of his stick.

I nodded.

Mark bent down to eye level with the eight ball to sight it into the pocket. He stepped to the other side of the table and did the same, looking from the pocket back toward the ball. He walked back to the cue ball and decided to chalk his stick. When he finished chalking, he stroked the cue several times, and double-checked the line from the eight ball, his pool rule version of the carpenter's adage to measure twice, cut once.

I lit a cigarette.

"She's really pretty," I said. "I gave her a flower from Ronaldo's entrance bouquet."

Mark walked back to the cue ball, held his cue at the ready long enough for me to take another swallow of beer, and then he shot. The eight ball went into the center of the hole and dropped into the corner pouch.

"Nice shot," I said.

I leaned my cue against the table, took a seat, and motioned to his beer.

Mark shot at one of my balls still on the table, sank it, shot at a second, but missed that one so he pushed it into the side pocket with his hand. Then he put the cue stick on the table and walked to his chair.

"You've never been any good with women," he said.

He snatched his pack of cigarettes from the table and took one. He liked using matches instead of a lighter because he said the sulfur made the tobacco taste better.

"And you're not going to be any good, not until you learn to be more aggressive," he said as he exhaled.

"I was aggressive. That's why she got fired."

"So far," he said, "you've told me you met a new woman whose name you do not know, you stole a flower from Ronaldo, a definite no-no, and because you were aggressive, this no name woman got fired."

"You've got it."

"Things couldn't be more clear."

"I wish I knew what to do."

"All right," he said, lifting his beer. "Tell me what happened."

I told him the whole story, explaining at last my uncertainty, because I didn't know how the flower ended up in the dishwasher, or why.

"I need a beer," he said.

He went to the bar and brought back two cold ones.

"Okay. First thing to do is get her job back."

"Me? How?"

"Talk to Ronaldo. He likes you. Just tell him what happened."

"Confess?"

"Confess."

"I'll lose my job."

"Not like you make enough to worry."

"Yeah."

"I got this new gig. Selling cars," Mark said. "I make as much on one sale as you make in two weeks. I could get you on. Beats washing dishes, believe me."

"I don't know, Mark. I don't really have the personality for sales. And used cars? I don't know."

"Shoot yourself," he said. "You want the girl, you got to risk. It's up to you."

I wasn't overjoyed at either of Mark's suggestions. I couldn't sell cars, I knew that. I didn't trust used car salesmen then, and I still don't. Besides, I didn't want to quit school, and I felt like I would stick to that no matter what. It's true that Ronaldo had been good to me, and Mark was right, Ronaldo liked me.

I straightened my back and sat forward in the chair.

"You're right, Mark. I've got to do what's right."

"I didn't say right. I said expedient."

"Yeah, yeah."

He nodded, drained his beer, and stood.

"Pay the man," he said.

"What are you talking about?"

"Pay Johnny."

He pointed to the table and smiled.

"You lost."

Chapter 4

Ronaldo forgave me.

"I understand love," he said. "But next time, ask."

"I will."

"And I'll tell you no."

I got the point.

The route to the meaning of the flower in the dish rack, however, proved serpentine. No one knew anything about it. As I prepared for the dinner rush, I checked the dish table and discovered two trays, one about half full of dirty water glasses and a flat tray with silverware. A dirty napkin and an ashtray full of butts rested on the silver, but they didn't belong there. Everybody knew. The bus-boys were supposed to separate dishes, glasses, and silver, and they were supposed to dump the trash and bag the dirty linen. After all, I couldn't do everything.

I checked around, and Ronaldo had hired a new part-time kid, Alec or Alex or something. Just a young guy, still in high school.

"Did you do that?" I asked him.

"Yeah. I guess I did."

"You're supposed to put the linen in the hampers and the trash in the containers. The dish trays are for dirty dishes."

"I know," he said. "I'm sorry. It got busy. I tried to get ahead of things by picking up as I went, and I left some things on the trays. I just forgot to take them off."

"You're not supposed to do that, either."

"I was just trying to help."

"I know it can get hectic, but that's why we have rules, so when everybody's busy, we all know what to do. Things run smoother that way."

"I understand."

"Good," I said.

"Is it okay if I go now? I've got to clean the waitress station before I go home."

"Sure. Go ahead."

He started toward the doorway.

"Hey, Alex, wait a minute."

"It's Allan," he said.

"Allan, the other day, did you happen to clean up the waitress area and pick up a flower? You know, one of those long stemmed ones? A calla lily?"

"Yes," he answered with some hesitancy. "It was laying on the shelf, and I figured it was spoiled or something. Why?"

"Because you left that on a bunch of dishes. If that went through the washer, the health department would get all over us. You've got to be more careful."

"Okay," he said. "I'm really sorry. I won't do it again."

"Okay," I said. "Try to remember."

She didn't reject the offer. I was psyched. Of course, I had to calm down and make a plan. I decided I would act aloof like Mark, relaxed, not over anxious, and not too energetic like I normally am.

About midnight, when the food business shrunk to appetizers and bar patrons, I waited until I noticed Charlene working on her book. I made a trip to the waitress station to pick up a tray of dirty glasses.

"Hey," I said. "Glad you're back."

"Thanks."

"I'm sorry about the trouble I caused you. Could we talk a minute before you leave?"

"What about?" she asked.

"Oh, you know, the flower, I guess."

"What about it?"

"Well, it's funny. Do you know how Ronaldo discovered the thing? The new bus-boy, Alex. . ."

"Allan," she corrected.

"Yeah, Allan. He picked it up from the station and left it on a tray. Ronaldo just happened to be back there when I pulled the tray."

She nodded, those inviting eyes as restless and permeating as a tide change. I stared into them and forgot to talk. She looked down and blinked, and her long black lashes seemed to close in slow motion like a rippled wave in a tidal pond.

Finally, she said, "That's very interesting."

"It is, isn't it?" I said. "So, I just wanted you to know."

"All right," she said. "But it was just a flower, and it

wasn't yours."

She picked up her order book and walked away.

She remained a puzzle, but I remained determined.

After work, I caught Charlene as she was leaving.

"I thought we were going to talk?"

"We already talked."

"Well, how about I give you a ride home?"

"Okay."

"Could you give me a couple of dollars for gas? Payday's not until Friday."

"My payday is Friday, too," she said, and walked to the bus kiosk.

Chapter 5

Mothers prophesy the future by creating it in their children. When I was young, my mother told me I was beautiful. Perhaps because she had no daughter, she chose to adorn me with a feminine adjective. I don't know. But how can a boy respond to something like that?

I had an easier time understanding and responding to my father. He'd say, "Clean the back yard, and don't give me any lip." Easy, simple, direct, clear. I could clean the yard or challenge him. If I challenged him, he'd explain the Darwinian concept of natural selection: that strength and size win out over youth and swagger.

But with mom, she'd hug me, and I could smell her, like summer sun-tea, and I'd feel safe, and she'd say, "You're my beautiful boy." You tell me how to rebel against that. No way. Nevertheless, such a slippery message encouraged neither strength nor aggression; it demanded compliance and obedience. So I grew up beautiful.

I explained this to Mark, concluding that Charlene's coldness toward me had nothing to do with a lack of physical attractiveness on my part. What, then, could it be?

"You need to get laid," he said.

I wasn't entirely certain that such a simple solution could resolve all emotional debate, and I said so.

"Look," he said, "I quit school, and I want to celebrate."

"You quit school?"

"Sure," he said. "I wasn't learning anything, and I'm making real money selling cars part time. Imagine what I'll do if I sell full time."

Mark wore a new, blue, silk shirt, a new pair of chinos, and a new pair of dark buckskin shoes. That wardrobe probably cost more than I earned in two weeks at the Bistro.

"If you think it's the best for you," I said. "But I can't go out. I'm broke."

"You're always broke, Danny boy, and it's time you smarten up."

"Oh?"

"Look. Quit school. Forget about falling in love. Get out in the real world and make some money."

Mark craved money like a great white greeds after a seal, and he often ambushed me into thinking my way out of problems by succumbing to pleasure. For him, life was simple: appetites demand fulfillment.

"Let's go out," he said, uncrossing his long legs and planting his new buckskins on the floor. "We'll have a few drinks and pick up some girls. That's the way to get over somebody. Remember, there's a billion women in the world."

Mark drove to The Bull Pen, a neighborhood bar with dart boards, pool tables, and four TVs. We sat in a booth where the waitress brought a pitcher, two glasses, and a big bowl of salty popcorn.

"I don't want to quit school," I said.

"Look at yourself, Daniel. You're good looking, smart, and young. That's what employers want. Youth. You'll get your real education on the job. Everybody knows that."

"Aren't you even a little afraid, Mark?"

He sipped his beer; then set the mug on the table. He put his long fingers together and touched the tip of his nose.

"I don't think so. My old man, he never went to school. But he was lucky. He bought that land by the river when it was cheap, and with the value of the house appreciating every week, he'll be okay. I want to be lucky and good," he said, emphasizing the word *and*. "Know what he said to me? Said I should eat more apples because apples prevent cancer."

He paused to chew on two pieces of popcorn. I watched his jaw muscles move, and although he kept his lips closed, I could see the outline of his tongue moving around to clean his teeth.

"I'll never be like him," he said, and he took a long drink of beer. "If I'm afraid of anything, it's that I'll end up like him. Yesterday, I felt great after I quit school, but last night that ghost showed up again and made the step squeak. Like it was looking for something."

He leaned toward me.

"Ghosts can't hurt you as long as you're not afraid of them. And I'm not afraid, 'cause only two things matter, money and sex. That's what real power is all about."

Doctor Leonard once told me that Mark's sensitivity to spirits constituted a gift so often misunderstood that sometimes those who have it are afraid to tell people because of ridicule. That is why I befriended Mark, he insisted. "You understand him," he assured me.

"There," Mark said, pointing to the bar.

Two blondes sat on stools designed to emphasize long legs.

"Wait here. I'm gonna take care of us."

Mark eased out of the booth. He stood next to the table, took a cigarette from the pack, and put it behind his ear. Then he strolled toward the women. He took his time, his gangly arms covered with shiny silk. He stopped behind them.

He waited for them to recognize his presence, and when they turned their heads toward him, he took the cigarette from his ear and put it in his mouth. He reached in his pocket to pull out a book of matches, not really ignoring the girls, but not talking to them either. He held the match between his fingers, cupped inside his hand like a high planes cowboy protecting the flame from wind. When he struck the match and it flamed, he made a circle out of his fingers and thumb and put the cigarette in the hole to light it. He opened his hand and waved away the flame like Will Rogers throwing a lariat. He took the cigarette from his mouth and exhaled a line of smoke over the heads of the women.

I watched him lower his head to say something to them, and one of them looked past Mark to me. The girl turned back to her friend, and Mark continued to talk.

Finally, the women both turned back to their drinks. Mark took a step back. With no change in demeanor, he inhaled deeply, pulled the cigarette away from his face, and exhaled a slow, intentional stream of smoke at the TV on the wall behind the bartender.

He returned to the booth and took his seat.

"They're busy," he said, and laid his cigarette in the ashtray. He tipped the pitcher, poured the last of the beer into his glass, and set the pitcher at the edge of the table so the waitress would know he wanted a refill.

"I don't know if I want another one, Mark," I said. "I've got two classes tomorrow, and I work tomorrow night."

"It's okay," he said. "I'm not done yet."

The waitress stopped. She picked up the empty pitcher.

"Another beer?" she asked.

Mark nodded.

"Anything else?"

"Yeah," Mark said. "Your phone number."

She looked at him in silence. She jerked her head toward me and quickly back to Mark.

"I don't think so," she said, and walked away.

When she returned with the beer, she set the pitcher in front of Mark. He gave her a five dollar bill and told her to keep the change.

"How about breakfast after you're done with work? I'll bet you're hungry by then," he tried again.

"No. But thanks anyway," she said.

Mark filled both our mugs.

"Cheers," he said, lifting the glass.

Mark had a way of smiling at defeat, an almost imperceptible grin behind his mouth as if he knew a secret no one else knew and he had every intention of keeping it to himself. I admired him for that. It seemed mature to me. I acted more like a puppy. If I liked something I showed it, and if something hurt me, I showed that too.

"What do you say we call it a night?" I said.

He looked at the half-empty pitcher and at his half-empty glass. He lifted the mug, drained the beer, and said, "Waste not, want not."

He lifted the pitcher and filled each of our glasses to the brim.

"To the hunt," he toasted.

We clanked glasses and emptied them.

Mark set his glass on the tabletop.

"You're right," he said. "Let's get out of here."

On the way out, I smiled at the girls at the bar. They did not smile back.

That night, I dreamt of Charlene. In the dream, I think I was smiling.

Chapter 6

I designed a foolproof plan to convince Charlene to go out with me.

Reverse psychology.

I asked one of the other waitresses, Odette Woodlin, to go dancing. It was fairly common knowledge that in order to get a woman interested in you, you had to pretend you were not interested in her. Why this attempt to trigger jealousy in order to induce affection held importance, I cannot say. The fact is, shooting an arrow to the left in order to hit the target on the right sounded more Zen than American, but California has a way of making the unusual common.

I did not tell Mark about my plan, but I did invite him to double date with us because Odette wanted to bring along her girlfriend, Tammy. We all met at The Plasma, a bar with a dance floor, full of students from Marysville College on Thursday, fifty cent beer night. Odette and Tammie were already on the floor.

I danced with Odette. Mark danced with Tammy.

When the DJ took a break, we went to a table along the side wall. The heat and exertion made us all sweat. Odette pushed her hair away from her eyes, and Tammie dabbed her cheeks with a napkin. Mark dragged his beer mug across his forehead, letting the condensation cool him.

"At least we can hear," I said.

Odette introduced Tammie, and Mark shook Tammie's hand. He stood to shake Odette's hand.

"And you must be Charlene," he said. "I'm happy to finally meet you."

Odette pulled her hand away and looked at him, surprised and perhaps hurt.

"I'm Odette," she said and exchanged glances with Tammie, glances which I interpreted as fatal to any further joviality.

"Mark, this is Odette. She works at The Bistro," I tried to explain, but Odette was not happy. Her face turned granite, and she folded her hands on her lap. Mark continued to stand, looking from face to face to face, but silent.

"Well?" Odette asked.

I might have blushed, but I think the darkness hid it.

"Well," I began, but I couldn't think of any good way to explain my reverse-psychology deception.

I glanced at Mark. He was obviously enjoying my predicament. He let me sweat for a couple more seconds, and then he spoke.

"Odette, it's my fault."

She looked at him, face unchanged, hands still on her lap.

"You see," Mark continued, "Daniel here has a thing for Charlene, and when he told me we were going out, I just figured he asked Charlene."

Then he turned to Tammie.

"And I really owe you an apology too, Tammie," he said, shifting his glance, all of us startled at the change. "You see, I thought you were Odette."

At that, even I looked puzzled.

"Daniel has told me a lot about you," he said, returning his attention to Odette. He leaned his torso closer to her. "In fact, I've been begging him for weeks to set something up so I could meet you. I just didn't know it was tonight."

He looked at me.

"You got me on this one, Danny boy. I only wish you had told me so I wouldn't have made such a mess of things."

He turned his attention to Odette again.

"Do you think we could start over, Odette? I'm not as messed up as it looks. Would you like to dance?"

Odette's face turned to supple sensuality.

"Daniel," she said, "you're bad. Why didn't you just tell me?"

She looked at Mark. "Okay, let's try again."

She stood, and Mark walked around the table to take her hand.

Tammie shook her head at me and drank some beer. When a tall guy with a moustache asked her to dance, she accepted.

Tammie went home with the tall moustache guy, and Odette went home with Mark.

Good thing I brought my own car.

The next evening at work, Odette announced that she found Mark interesting and that I had the hots for Charlene. I felt so embarrassed that I turned the water temperature beyond one hundred and forty degrees so that I could hide behind the dishwasher's protective shroud of steam. From time to time, I pierced the fog and watched first one, and then another, of the waitresses band together around Odette or Charlene, full of smiles and pointing in my direction.

As luck would have it, Odette and Charlene became best friends.

Chapter 7

Under the pressure of sincere wooing on my part, Charlene finally agreed to go out with me. However, my dating acumen lacked some sophistication, so I obeyed the instructions of dating etiquette I learned from the lessons provided on nighttime television, to be fashionably late, and to bring your first date to a fancy restaurant you cannot really afford.

I picked up Charlene at her small apartment at exactly 7:09 pm, nine minutes later than the time we agreed on, and then I drove us to Miller's, a fancy restaurant with a reputation for excellent steaks, a place I could not afford.

I phoned ahead for a reservation, a gesture intended to impress Charlene almost as much as the food prices.

At the entrance, I announced, "Reed. Party of two."

The maître de sat us at a square table with a white linen cloth cover and white linen napkins with two forks on them. They even provided a special small knife with the butter dish.

I watched Charlene unfold her napkin and place it on her lap. She watched me watching her, and she smiled. I felt certain we would both remember this night.

A sub-waiter brought glasses of ice water, and the table waiter pushed a small cart with a bottle of house red in a green bottle, iced within a silver glacette. He poured a sipping portion of the wine into each wine glass. I lifted the

33

glass to my nose, inhaled the red bouquet, and sipped a small amount, inhaling a prolonged breath over the wine to enjoy the subtle flavors of oak and mountain grape at the back of my tongue. Then I swallowed its gentle fire down my throat, past my esophagus, and into my belly. I'm pretty sure Charlene was impressed.

"Excellent," I said, and placed the wine glass on the table so he could fill it.

He turned to Charlene. She smiled, and the waiter, obviously taken by her beauty, bowed toward her.

"None for me, thank you. I don't drink."

The waiter nodded and returned the bottle to the glacette, providing me the opportunity to pour my own.

Charlene ordered the salmon with sauce. I ordered a T-bone, well-done.

To break an awkward silence, I asked, "Do you like this place?"

"It's nice," she said. "How is school going?"

Funny, as I recollect, how Charlene turned our conversation away from herself and back to me. Of course, I could always complain about school to anyone willing to listen, and I talked nearly non-stop, pausing from time to time to eat portions of the cold bean salad. Charlene sat quietly, inviting me to talk more.

I slipped imperceptibly into a short discourse on my business ambitions, once I finished college. Before I got to the part where I would become a millionaire, the main courses arrived. We both took a moment to admire the presentation. I cut a chunk of the steak, and when I tasted it, I mumbled a soft groan.

Charlene took a small forkful of garlic potatoes and raised her eyebrows in an expression of approval. She placed her fork against the dish and lifted the napkin from her lap.

"I need to go powder my nose," she said.

I had a mouthful of carrots sweetened with brown sugar, so I nodded.

The steak was as good as advertised. I enjoyed one moist, perfectly cooked forkful after another. The juices and spices and meaty texture blended to encourage a sort of T-bone engorgement. It did not take long to finish the steak, and I felt tempted to pick up the bone and gnaw it, but I restrained this impulse. I finished the last two carrots and left the broccoli.

I was pouring another glass of wine when Charlene returned to the table. She lifted her fork and broke off a piece of the salmon. I watched her lips surround the fork as the fish disappeared. She stared back at me, trying to chew and smile simultaneously. She managed another piece of salmon and two forksful of potatoes, and all the while I did not take my eyes from her.

Finally, she said, "I'm getting full. Let's get a box, and I'll take the rest with me."

I thought that for a person who doesn't drink, she sure

doesn't eat much either.

I gave the waiter a little extra because we had such a beautiful evening.

When we reached her apartment, I asked her, "Did you enjoy dinner?"

"Yes, I did, Daniel," she said. "Thank you."

"You're welcome. That's a great place, isn't it?"

"Yes, it is."

"Maybe we can do it again sometime?"

"Probably," she said. "But, Daniel, it is polite to wait to eat until a woman has returned from powdering her nose."

Chapter 8

Charlene and I became an item, as they say, and over the next few months, with Mark and Odette dating, the four of us often spent evenings together. We didn't go out much, though, mostly because I had to study, and, besides, I didn't have much money to spend on dates. Charlene didn't mind, but Mark did.

One Wednesday afternoon, he sauntered into my place. I didn't work that night because I had finals and Ronaldo let me cut my hours at the end of semester so I could study.

"Nothing personal," Mark said, "but we've got to go out, do something."

"I'm trying to study," I said.

Mark sat in the middle of the couch and spread his long arms across the backrest. He looked slowly around the room, especially at the ceiling, making an appraisal like a disappointed architectural judge.

"I've got a plan," he said.

"Tell someone else. I'm trying to study."

"When are finals?"

"Next week."

"Then what?"

"Same as always. Work as many hours as I can to save some cash for next semester."

"That's what I'm talking about. The rat race is getting to you. Same four walls, and by the way your ceiling is dirty.

Too much school. Too much work. You've forgotten how to play, Danny boy, so me and Odette are inviting you and Charlene to go skiing next weekend. After your last final."

"Can't. No money. Got to work. Never skied."

"All taken care of, amigo. Ski resort at Donner Pass. My treat. Rented a room for four. Of course, you and Charlene have to cover your own food and drinks. Odette talked to Ronaldo, and he said have a good time. That old guy really likes you. You should take advantage of it sometime."

"You're kidding."

"Nope. We're going skiing. Wouldn't you know, Odette's a skier, too. I'm surprised at how much we have in common." He paused a moment. "You know, I think I'm beginning to like her."

"You?"

He ignored me, uncrossed his legs, and lit a cigarette. He pulled the ashtray from the coffee table and put it on the arm of the couch.

"It's time you learned how to ski," he said, and the matter was settled.

We took Odette's car. She cinched the ski equipment on the roof, organized the luggage in the trunk, and arranged four people in the seats, she and Mark in front, Charlene and me in the back.

The drive through Truckee took us into a swirling white radiance, the falling snow silent yet startling. Trees anchored to granite mountains loomed like giant gatekeepers. The sun accentuated the vast whiteness and highlighted the blue sky, a background to high, billowing clouds. The wind stirred the branches of the trees, and their movements looked intentional.

"It's beautiful up here," I said.

Charlene held my arm and rested her head on my shoulder.

They rented a cottage near the back of the development, set in the forest, with a ski path to the lifts and a walking path to the main lodge. The cottage had two bedrooms, two bathrooms, and a great room with a TV, a microwave, a refrigerator, and a small bar with a polished top cut from a two inch thick slab of redwood. The deep carpet felt soft, even wearing shoes.

Mark prepared to get a fire going, but Odette stopped him.

"Don't do that," she said.

"Why?"

"I want to ski, and I want a big meal in the restaurant when we're done."

He nodded, and they dragged Charlene and me to the rental area to get boots, skis, and poles.

"What do you think?" I asked Charlene.

"I'm excited."

"Me too."

Everything went well until I shifted from the wooden planks of the ski shop to the snow covered earth. I'd never thought about it, but skis hold pretty well to dry wood, and when they hit snow, they slide. Mine slid faster than my body, and my feet took off ahead of my torso. When my body hit the ground, the skis halted. Everyone thought it was funny, except me.

Mark helped me up, and Odette tried to show me how to slide, using a gliding motion of the hips rather than the lift-step-land motion of walking.

She laughed at my efforts, and then she comforted me. "You'll get the hang of it."

Mark demonstrated the same technique to Charlene, and she glided off toward the bunny run.

"They have a dry school here, Daniel," Odette said.

"What's that?"

"An instructor will teach you the basics on a carpeted area. You won't slip, like on the snow, and it will really help your confidence."

"You think it will help?"

"Sure. It's your first time. Most people don't get it their first time out."

"Looks like Charlene did."

"Yes. Well, we'll see how she does. Most people will benefit from the dry ski school. I think you will too."

I accepted this minor embarrassment as necessary prelude to excellence, and I plodded my way to the dry ski school to learn how to ski on carpet.

Charlene decided to allow Mark and Odette to coach

her, so they gathered at the bunny slope.

Dry ski school demands focus and courage, and before long I actually stood at the top of the carpeted hill ready to risk the slope. The instructor encouraged me to bend at the knees, lean forward, and push away with the poles.

I did.

I flew down that carpeted mountain so fast I could not see a single object clearly, only blurs. At the bottom, I slowed down, and with minor stumbling came to a stop without falling.

The instructor hurried to my side.

"That was great," she said. "Let's get up there and try it again."

I turned, using the slow lift-place – lift-place technique. After four or five steps, I looked at the carpeted hill, ominously steep, and decided that I would put my formidable talents to better use in the bar.

I met a fine barkeep named Denny who never asked one question about my skiing experience. In recognition of this favor, I tipped him more than I could afford, and he doubled up the scotches for me. By the time my friends returned from the slopes, I needed some assistance getting back to the cottage.

They all dressed for dinner, and before they left, Charlene put me to bed. I remember saying good night to her.

The next thing I remember she was shaking me awake.

"Daniel," she said. "Daniel, wake up."

I opened one eye.

"We're near Donner Pass."

"Okay," I said.

"Why did you bring me to the place where those people ate each other?"

"Okay," I repeated and went back to sleep.

In the morning, the sun rose before I did.

When I did get out of bed, I discovered an empty cottage. It wasn't too late, ten-thirty maybe, but obviously the others started early. I dressed, enjoyed a late breakfast, and took the walk-path to the rest area at the top of the beginner's trail. I hurried inside, where the skiers and visitors like me could warm up and get some cocoa or a burger. Beyond the serving area, chairs and tables were arranged in a big room with half walls all the way around so people could watch the skiers. I bought some cocoa, sat at a table, and tried to find Charlene.

Eventually, I saw her and Mark together on a little ridge. I watched them talk. Mark pointed, Charlene nodded. Then Charlene pointed, and Mark nodded. They dug their poles into the snow and took off down the hill headed toward the rest area.

Charlene never skied before, so it surprised me to watch her glide through the snow as fearless as a six year old on a slip-and-slide.

Their run ended about twenty yards away, and I went

outside to meet them.

"Hey, you guys," I shouted. "How about some cocoa?"

Charlene nodded recognition. Her white skin shone, and tiny pink rosettes highlighted her cheeks.

Mark smiled too. He looked happy, as if he'd forgotten his need for superiority. Charlene could do that, allow people to drop pretenses and enjoy themselves. Maybe that's why she was such a good waitress.

Charlene and Mark removed their skis and walked to an empty table, while I ordered three cups of cocoa.

As I set the plastic tray before them, Mark and Charlene both rubbed their hands like children.

Mark lit a cigarette.

"You did pretty good," he told Charlene. Then he turned to me. "I told you to let me teach you. You might be as good as her in a season or two."

I sipped my cocoa, knowing I had no satisfactory comeback. Charlene, however, did.

"I think Daniel could ski fine if he wanted to."

"Not so," Mark said. "Got to have talent and coaching. And," he added, "experience."

"I think it's mental," Charlene corrected him.

"Maybe in races between good skiers," Mark suggested. "Good skiers of equal talent and experience. Like between Odette and me."

Odette had gone to the black diamond slope.

"Well," Charlene demurred, "you might think so, but I

still say it's mental." She sipped her cocoa. "I guess we'll never know."

Mark stubbed his cigarette. He could not pass up a challenge.

"There is one way to know," he said. "We can race."

"Come on, Mark," I said. "It's her first day skiing."

"Second," he corrected. "Well?" he asked, his eyebrows raised.

"What do you have in mind?" Charlene asked.

"We've been skiing the beginner's slope, and because you're still new at it, we can't go for a black diamond run. But there are two trails between beginning and expert, the blue runs. We could race one of them."

"Hold on," I said. "She's never even seen a blue run. That's not a fair race."

"Proves my point," Mark answered.

"Doesn't prove anything," I said.

"Don't pay any attention to him, Charlene," Mark said. "He gets this way sometimes."

"Okay," she said.

"Okay?" Mark and I both repeated.

"Yes." She stood. "Let's go."

"Wait," I said. "Let's have lunch and talk about this."

But they were already buckling their skis.

This experience furthered my education. I learned that when Charlene put her mind to something, it was a done deal. Nevertheless, uneasiness disturbed my long return to the lodge. I didn't think Mark would hurt Charlene, knowing that his competitive strain did not extend to violence. I could not, however, say the same for the mountain. The inanimate nature of the thing did not distinguish between amateur and expert.

A mild wind gusted, and shards of icy flakes stung my face. A bright sun intensified the whiteness of the snow, and I hurried the last few steps into the lodge. I brushed the snow from my jacket and hung it on a wall hook. I stamped the snow from my boots and sat down on a wooden bench. I don't know why I felt compelled to protect Charlene, but I did, and I decided that this would be the last skiing expedition Charlene and I would make. It was simply too dangerous.

I felt better after reaching that conclusion, and I headed to the bar.

When Denny saw me, he saluted. I ordered a Kahlua to help warm my innards. I looked around for a seat, and I saw Odette across the way. She sat in front of one of the great windows which overlooked the mountainside. There were three empty chairs around the table, so I guess she expected us.

Odette's face contained no single remarkable feature. Two eyes, a nose, the regular. But each feature matched harmoniously so that a womanly knowledge shone beneath her warm smile. She wore a knitted sweater and wool leggings. She gave the impression that silence suited her.

"Done already?" I asked.

"Daniel," she said.

"Charlene and Mark are still out there." I pointed toward the middle of the hill.

"I think they're on their way in. Mark just finished, and Charlene came past just as you were sitting down. She looked pretty good for her first time."

"You sure she was ahead of Mark?" I asked.

"Yes. Why?"

"They were racing."

"Really?"

"Yeah. Mark said no new skier could beat an experienced one. And Charlene said it was all in his head, or her head, I'm not sure which. And then they got all goofy, and before I knew it, they took off."

"I think Charlene won."

By the time Odette and I finished our drinks, Charlene and Mark showed up, both their faces flushed from the cold. Charlene smiled and waved. Mark did not. They stopped at the bar. I could see Mark needed a scotch, perhaps a double. Charlene drank soda.

They sat down, all of us silent. Charlene sipped her soda. Mark gulped his drink. Odette and I waited.

Finally, Mark put his glass down.

"I didn't lose," he said. "I fell, so it doesn't count."

"What happened?" Odette asked.

"I was way ahead, and I flew off a mogul beautifully, but

I landed on ice. You know that's not fair. I lost control and fell. That's why she got down before me, but she didn't beat me."

"Were you hurt?"

"No."

Suddenly, I had the image of Mark lifting off a mogul trying to keep his naturally uncoordinated body under control, then hitting an ice patch and him all akimbo, plopping eventually in a snow pile. The image made me grin.

Charlene noticed, and whispered, "It was fun."

I realized she'd discovered a new sport and I'd be spending more time at this ski lodge than I might like.

Mark complained to Odette, "No woman can beat me."

"There, there," she said, but she was smiling too.

I think Mark noticed.

Chapter 9

A couple of weeks later, an abnormal situation occurred at The Bistro. Ronaldo was late.

I arrived early that day. We always drew large crowds leading up to Christmas, and I worked all the extra hours I could for the coming semester. I wanted to get a few things ready. Soap, extra dishes to replace breakage, things like that. Odette was already there, too. She had been working for Ronaldo longer than me, and she knew the routine. We waved but didn't speak.

The atmosphere felt busy; not rushed or disorderly, just a good sense of work to do and people getting things done.

Sometime around three-thirty, Ronaldo's wife Patricia walked in. She brought Ronaldo's evening suit and a clean white shirt. As she headed toward the office, she waved to me, and she said hello to everyone she passed. I didn't realize Ronaldo hadn't shown up yet.

The early dinner crowd began to arrive about five o'clock. Ronaldo rushed in at ten minutes in front of five. He hastened to the office, but he and Patricia stayed behind the closed door. Odette acted as hostess, seating two groups of early arrivals. At five-thirty she decided to knock on the office door.

"Ronaldo. Patricia," she said. "It's five-thirty, and people are here."

The door opened, and Ronaldo and Patricia came out,

blushing slightly like two teenagers.

"Thank you, Odette," Ronaldo said.

He walked to the entrance podium, and Patricia began to visit the patrons.

Patricia knew all the steady customers by name and the names of their kids and where they went to school. She wore an expensive but modest dress and low heeled shoes. She had long feet and toes, and at fifty, she walked with the pace of a matron. She visited every table at least once each evening, and in the process of friendly conversation, she found out how well the servers behaved and if the food met with each person's approval. She felt no qualms about returning an underdone steak or an overcooked potato. Everyone knew she held the power in the marriage, and the sophisticated atmosphere of the restaurant ensued entirely from her.

Ronaldo adored her. Perhaps one of the notable personality quirks of the Bistro occurred because of Ronaldo's flirtatious attention to his wife. When they passed each other he smiled at her, and sometimes they touched hands. It wasn't your average restaurant in that sense; they made people feel like they were visiting friends.

I didn't sense anything out of the ordinary until nine-thirty or so when I suddenly realized I hadn't seen Charlene. I took a quick break and tracked down Odette.

"Where's Charlene?" I asked.

"She's at my place," Odette told me.

"Is she sick?"

"No."

"Why isn't she at work?"

"She quit."

"She quit? Why would she do that?"

"I'll let her tell you. I'm not sure about it at all, Daniel. It just doesn't make sense."

"Of course not. How is she going to get by? Pay her rent? Eat?"

A customer motioned for her. "I've got to go," Odette said. "You can talk to her yourself."

I couldn't dwell on the conversation because dirty dishes continued in a steady flow. I reasoned that some small occurrence upset Charlene, and we'd find a solution.

After work, I drove to Odette's apartment. A light shone from the window. Odette let me in, and without saying a word, she went to bed. Charlene sat on the couch. She held a cup of tea in both hands. She blew across the top of the cup, and a tiny bellow of steam tumbled away from her lips. She took a cautious sip.

"Good," she said.

"Tell me what happened," I said.

"I quit."

"I know, Char, but why?"

"He made a pass at me."

"Who?"

"Ronaldo."

"Ronaldo? That doesn't sound like him."

"That's what Odette said."

She looked at the top of the brew, then lifted the cup and drank.

"Charlene, I don't think anyone has ever accused Ronaldo of anything like that. Tell me what happened."

"When I picked up my check today, the amount seemed wrong so I called the accountant. Ronaldo answered the phone, and he told me to come over. He said we could straighten out any problem."

She sipped the tea.

"And?"

"When I got there, the accountant was gone, and Ronaldo grabbed me and pulled me into a room with a couch."

"He did?"

"He did. He told me again that we could fix any problem we might have, and then he tried to unbutton my blouse."

"I don't believe it," I said.

"Then you don't love me," she said. "Get out."

"That's not what I mean, Charlene. I believe you. I just can't believe Ronaldo would act like that because, well, no one's ever suggested anything like it."

"It happened anyway," she said. "And I told him I quit. Then I told my landlady I had to move. I have to be out by the end of the month. Odette said I could stay here if I need to. Until I find something."

"That could take a while. What about work?"

She raised her eyebrows and shrugged.

"Think you can find a job and rent a place in two weeks?"

She continued in silence, looking from the teacup to me.

I had been thinking about us moving in together, but whenever I brought it up, Charlene seemed reluctant. She considered it a big move.

"Why don't you move in with me? It might be a good time."

"Are you asking me?"

"Yes. I'm asking you."

"Then, yes, Daniel," she said. "I will marry you."

And that settled it.

Chapter 10

Marriage ceremonies in California mirror the participants. Some people sky dive, others fly off in a hot air balloon. Some people get married in front of a Justice of the Peace.

Until that morning, in the first week of the new year and the beginning of our new lives together, I never thought about justice and peace having anything to do with one another. Justice seems firm, even military, and peace seems dove like or Haight-Ashbury. I decided that if there's justice in a marriage, then there can also be peace. I asked Mark what he thought as he drove us all to the Church, but he rolled down the window and exhaled cigarette smoke out his nose into the wind.

Maybe I was nervous and needed to talk. I've heard it's not uncommon to feel nervous before getting married. Charlene and Odette talked in the back seat. I didn't listen to the words, just recognized the hum of their voices, Odette's school-teacher's efficient voice and Charlene's sometimes girlish giggle when something made her laugh.

I wasn't afraid, but I did feel a cautionary rumble in the center of my stomach. It felt like I'd swallowed ten or eleven red cherries with the pits still in them. I closed my eyes, and the sound of the girls' voices, and the rumble of trucks outside the window, and the mild thunder of the wind blowing through the open window blended in my ears like peanut butter and maple syrup. Inside my head, a vision of fifty years of bliss with Charlene. Husband and wife. Till death do us part.

Like I said, I was probably nervous.

St. Michael's Church had a long walk to the vestibule. We knocked, and Fr. Jardine let us in. Odette and Mark filled out most of the paperwork, they being the maid of honor and the best man. They looked beautiful. Odette wore a three-quarter length dress of red chemise with a cloth belt around her waist. She wore matching red heels which emphasized her calves. She possessed legs models pay plastic surgeons to build, long and muscular at the calf and dancer-thin at the ankles. Mark wore a three-quarter length, black leather jacket with twill pants and black patent leather loafers. He also wore a thin gold chain around his neck. They made a perfect couple.

Charlene and I both wore jeans, so we matched. I did wear a blue tie with a matching blue shirt. Charlene wore a sleeveless blouse. She carried a bride's bouquet of Lilies of the Field.

We did not compose vows. Instead, we asked Fr. Jardine to use the traditional promises. "For better or for worse." "For richer and for poorer." "In sickness and in health." Public declarations of commitment, made to honor human laws cloaked within the envelope of spiritual grace. With each phrase, Charlene and I looked at each other, love-struck, nodding as if to prophesy the certainty of our earthly life commitment. Formal. Intentional. "Till death do us part."

After we said, "I do," Charlene threw her bouquet to Odette. Odette caught the bouquet. I kissed Charlene. Odette kissed Mark. And thus did the blessed adventure of our marriage begin.

Chapter 11

Our marriage reception was neither large nor expensive. Mark and Odette brought a bottle of champagne and a box of fried chicken to the apartment.

"To your new life," Mark toasted.

We drank, giddy with the simplicity of faith that actions taken represent expectations fulfilled. We did not know that the future possesses vast caverns of uncertainty. Nor did we care. The truth is we had little certainty except a hopefulness that our friendships would endure.

"To my love," I proposed, and we drank. Even Charlene enjoyed one glass.

When we finished the bottle of champagne, Mark and Odette left.

The reality of the moment struck as the door closed, the click of the latch firm and final. The end of our single lives.

"We're married," I said.

She held my hand, and we walked toward the bedroom. We needed no more words.

Just before she stepped over the threshold, Charlene stopped.

"We can't make love in your bed," she said.

"What's wrong?"

"Daniel, it's a mess in there."

I had lived alone long enough that the messiness of my lifestyle did not cause consternation on my part, so her outsider's observation of it surprised me.

"Let me straighten things."

I shook the blanket, tightened the sheets, and fluffed the pillows.

"There," I said, and gestured an invitation.

"I don't know how you sleep on this thing." She shook her head. "I can't."

Normally, one might attempt analysis or compromise, but this was our wedding night, and, frankly, I had no idea how to respond.

We sat on the couch.

"What?"

"The bed has to go," she said.

"It's too late to buy a new one. The stores are closed."

"Tomorrow. First thing."

"Okay."

"Do you want to sleep here?"

We had snuggled enough on that old couch, so it was familiar. We initiated an earnest attempt, but in the enthusiasm of our wedding night explorations, we fell onto the floor.

Charlene laughed, which surprised me, and I laughed too, which surprised me, and we sat with our backs against the couch in the comfort of the humor that brought the enormity of marriage to a manageable moment.

"What now?" I asked.

"We must make our bed."

"So," I suggested, "we must make our own bed and lay in it."

"Exactly," she said. "We shall lay blankets on the floor and make our own wedding bed, like in the fairy tales."

The absurdity of the suggestion seemed to hit us both at the same time. Naturally, we jumped up immediately to gather resources.

Circumstances had grown beyond care, and the newness of our future delighted us. We constructed a place to lay with deliberation and folly. As the act of making our marriage bed took hold, it somehow connected us to the mysteries of the ancient communities of our human tribe, beyond any formality, any civil action. It became the culminating ceremony of our vows.

We placed three blankets, one on top of the next, on the living room floor in a square pattern, parallel to the north wall. But it felt foreign to the room, and I circled it as I might have circled a sacred fire. I pulled the edge to move it three inches away from the wall. I fluffed one pillow and threw it to the center of the blankets like an elven talisman. Then another.

I tiptoed away, backing up to get a fuller view.

Charlene stepped to my side. She cocked her head slightly as she analyzed the pattern and the choice of cloth.

"What do you judge?" I asked.

"It might work," she said, but she said it with a look of ironic pleasure, with fire in her eyes, like a fire-breathing full moon on a cloudless night.

We undressed, sitting next to one another on the couch.

I reached for her, and in that first naked married kiss her smell filled my nostrils, an aroma of closeness, the scent of spring leaves held against rain. The memory of it has never left me.

The pliant suction of her lips, the erection of her nipples, the flow of her juices triggered the nerves of my skin and my muscles and cinched the tension of my belly so tight I felt like a forest, sturdy, fecund, and vital beyond the timelessness of water. We slid to the floor, to the patterned blankets and the haphazard pillows. Our moans filled the room like the fall of water fills the chamber of a gorge. Entwined and eager, we held each other, and in that one living moment of unrestricted passion, totally enmeshed one within the other, we grew beyond the bed, beyond the room, beyond the forest and the sky, into that tundra of matrimonial union barren of all except the exquisite explosion of the sacred and unbridled fervor of the first night of a life-long, life-filled marriage.

We luxuriated in that endorphin-fueled, shared peacefulness of exhausted energy. Charlene pressed her face into the skin of my shoulder, and I held her with both my arms. The culmination of this singular day lay upon us like tenderness, and I wanted to stay wrapped in this comfort forever.

Chapter 12

The next day, we bought a mattress set, fitted sheets, two pillows, and pillowcases. I anticipated that we would purchase a king size bed. Not a waterbed, of course; they had become passé. But California does king size better than Chicago does skyscraper, and I figured, well, you know, when in Rome buy a king sized bed. I headed directly to the king size bed display.

What matter, a mattress? A simple sleeping tool, yes? Better than the floor. Well, mostly better than the floor. Yet, not just a place to sleep; a place to rest, a secure place where we will grow close to one another. Lost in these considerations, I asked Charlene, "Which one do you like?"

I failed to notice that Charlene had gone to the double mattress show area. I discovered her absence when she did not answer my question.

I went to her.

"Well?"

"This one," she said.

"But, Charlene, that's a double bed. Don't you want a king size? Big? Plenty of room?"

"No. A small bed will keep us close. A big bed will keep us apart. Plenty of room is too much room."

We bought the double bed, and each night as we slept on that new bed, I grew accustomed to her close to me, her warmth, her breath.

Chapter 13

As Charlene and I began to absorb the lessons of compromise required of marriage, our first dilemma occurred when Charlene told me she'd found a new place for us to live.

"What's wrong with this place?" I asked.

"I can't live here anymore."

"Why?"

"It's not safe."

"Not safe?"

"I'll show you."

She walked to the living room and pointed to the small fireplace in the center of the wall, a red brick façade, a matching brick hearth, and a painted wooden mantel.

"Do you see it?" she asked.

I looked at the firebrick in the burn area, yellow and tightly mortared, with black smudges from smoke outside the fire range. The red brick veneer looked sooty, but sturdy and safe. Although the burn of log fires left a shadow of grit above and along the sides of the mantel, the plastered walls appeared in good shape.

I don't see anything," I said.

Charlene stepped onto the hearth and put her finger to her lips.

"Shhhh," she whispered.

Then she pointed to a smoke stain on the wall. She

65

would not touch it. She backed away, keeping her face to the wall until she stood next to me.

"That's where he lives. Inside the shadow."

"Who?"

"His name is Captain. Sometimes when you're at school, he comes out all smoky and formless. Yesterday I asked him what he wanted. He told me, 'You can move the ball. Concentrate.' So I did it."

"What ball? What are you talking about?"

"Stop, Daniel. Listen to me."

She clutched her hands together.

"I rolled the softball with my mind. I rolled it across the floor. Last night, when you were at work, I was in bed reading. Suddenly, I looked away from the book to the door. Then I made the door close."

"That sounds pretty amazing, Char. I've seen psychokinesis on TV. I'm not sure I understand it, but I guess the mind can be pretty powerful. Can you do it now?"

"What?"

"Roll the ball?"

"No. And I don't want to."

"Close the door?"

"He's evil, Daniel. We must leave or he'll make me crazy. He wants our baby."

"Charlene, we don't have a baby."

"When I misbehaved, my father locked me in a closet. It was dark in there, and I was afraid, and I said, 'please, don't put me in there.' But he didn't listen. The only reason I survived is because the Captain protected me. He told me to be quiet and to concentrate on the light inside my eyes, right here behind the top of my nose. And I did. Then my father would open the door, and I would hug him and tell him I was sorry. He would explain that he put me in the darkness because he loved me, that the darkness would help me to think about being good. But the Captain told me not to think about anything, only the light in my eyes and how time could turn black like the darkness, and if there was no light then there was no time, and time would go away so I only stayed in the closet for an instant."

She stopped and looked around the room. She lit a cigarette and inhaled and exhaled the smoke with a loud sigh. I waited for her to speak again, but she did not.

"Honey, that's awful. You've never told me that story before."

"Yes, I have," she said. "You never listen to me."

"That's not true, Charlene. I would have remembered that."

"It doesn't matter. When I left my father's home, I told the Captain to stay there. But he's angry that I told him to stay away from me, and now that I'm going to have a baby, he wants my baby because he can't have me. He lives in this house now, and we can't stay here."

"When did you find out you are pregnant?"

That information surprised me even more than the fact

that she could close a door with her mind.

"You see," she said, "you never listen to me. I'm going to be pregnant after we move. So, we must move."

"Oh," I said.

She found a two bedroom house near the edge of the city, but not in the country, a medium-sized subdivision of single story homes built after World War II, sometime in the early 1950s. It did not have a garage. Instead, the builders added a carport on the east side. A six foot cedar fence enclosed the back yard, like all proper California neighborhoods, keeping privacy confined to length, width, and depth, and neighborliness to a minimum.

What is a house if not the setting where powers display? I happily let Charlene establish the rules in our new home. I encouraged it. I wanted her to feel safe. Sometimes she seemed too fragile for harsh words or harsh detergent, and although I admit that I did more dishes at The Bistro than at home, I did help as much as possible given work and school.

She accepted the leadership role in our marriage as if it were a natural consequence of birth. We arranged the furniture to her liking.

"Let's put the couch against the wall," she said.

I lifted one end and shuffled, then lifted the other end and shuffled, until I eased it against the wall.

Charlene held her elbow in one hand. She leaned her head one way, then the other.

"It's too far this way," she pointed. "It needs to be closer to the window."

She knew what she wanted, how she wanted the house to feel, what emotions she wanted from each piece of furniture and from each room. She wanted her home to reflect her.

I moved the couch again.

Chapter 14

In the second week of the new semester, a surprising feeling of unexplainable jubilation filled me as I walked out of my afternoon accounting class. I had begun my junior year in college, and I drove toward home comforted by that feeling of surprising joy, although I did not know its origin. The early autumn sun shone bright, and the muted orange hue softened the colors of the passing landscape like a background shadow in a da Vinci portrait. The earth released her spirits into the trees, and as if engaged in a momentary fit of signs and wonders, the trees whispered music. They sang to me.

Doctor Leonard assured me that such impressions expressed my unconscious awareness of Charlene's illness, like some husbands feel sympathy pains during a wife's pregnancy. "I helped a man whose breasts developed during his wife's pregnancy," Doctor Leonard told me. "Grew soft and palpable. Almost to the point of needing a bra."

He sucked on his pipe in a meditative posture.

"Yes," he said, and pulled the pipe from his mouth. "A strapping young man with a woman's breasts."

"How did you fix him?" I asked.

"Yes?"

"How did you cure him?"

"I explained the psychological connection, what we call

Couvade Syndrome, of course, and I admonished him that since he could not, as a man, lactate, he should recognize the subsummation for what it was."

"That cured him?"

"I believe so. Although when his nipples began leaking in response to his infant's cries, he stopped coming to see me."

"Oh."

"I would have enjoyed seeing that, actually," he said, patting his pipe with a fingertip.

I left him staring out the window, imagining whatever his imagination could make of a man with lactating breasts.

I'm still comfortable with omens, and that afternoon, driving home, the odd peach color along the horizon, and the fading softness of the trees preparing for the coming solstice, did, indeed, make me sing. I parked the car in the driveway and retrieved my books from the back seat. I had three hours to study before leaving for work.

Charlene met me at the door. Sometimes when I looked at her, I fell in love all over again. When she smiled, my eyes saw only her for that instant, and the rest of the world disappeared. "Hurry," she said. "I have a surprise."

She clutched my arm and walked me through the hall toward the kitchen. She stopped at the doorway and gestured at a newly arrived Sears oak pedestal dining table and four matching chairs.

"Isn't it wonderful?" she said. "I'm pregnant."

Chapter 15

Hope in this world rejuvenates with the expectation of birth. An infant changes all the lives around it. Each newborn invites maturity to youth, continuation to community, and hope to the world at large. Almost all humans know this as primordial certainty, preservation of the species, and the imperatives of maternal and paternal instincts. American retailers expand on these natural inclinations by insisting that the continuance of the species depends greatly upon the accumulation of manufactured necessities. These necessities, of course, bring expenses. The economics of childbirth, however, are not innate. They accrue as cultural inducements, and all practical aspects of them remain excluded from textbook learning. I should know. I almost graduated from college with a degree in business, and not one professor ever explained the practical aspects of having a baby.

As a person of intuition and insight, Charlene marched into motherhood with zesty exuberance. She prepared for this birth as no mother before her.

She began by painting the second bedroom, now the baby's room, pink.

"Why pink?" I asked.

"Because we're having a daughter."

"And you know this how?"

"Don't be silly," she laughed.

I did not intend the question as humor, and as I moved closer to her to discuss the technique of her prophetic vision, I kicked the paint can, and a splash of pink wall color landed on the carpet.

I grabbed a rag to clean the mess, but if you don't know already, paint on carpet produces an unremovable stain.

"It's not a problem," Charlene declared. "That carpet doesn't go with the room anyway."

"Oh?"

She smiled, forgiving my clumsiness.

"We'll buy new."

And she did.

The new carpet, a light gray, added a feminine, cool comfort to the room. It was our baby daughter's room, and I felt it.

That next Tuesday, on the way home from school, I stopped at the secondhand store to look at baby furniture. A couple of beds; a used mattress that smelled clean; but in a corner, behind a plastic rocking horse, I discovered a wooden cradle.

"It looks handmade," I said.

"Yes, it is," the saleswoman said. "Not many people notice."

"I want it. Will you hold it for me? I need to talk with Charlene."

"Of course."

After dinner, we sat on the couch in the living room.

Charlene sipped tea.

"I found a cradle at the secondhand store. It's handmade. It's perfect for our baby."

Charlene put her teacup on the side table.

"Daniel, we need a cradle, of course," she began, "but do we have to buy secondhand? I don't want Ella to live in someone else's furniture."

I did not remind her that all of my furniture was secondhand, the couch we sat on was secondhand, and the table holding her teacup. Of course, we slept on a new mattress, with a new bed frame, and we had just finished eating at a new dining table while sitting on new dining room chairs. As I thought about it, I liked the new furniture, and, truthfully, the difference between new and used managed, in some hazy way, to represent a perception of security within our home. As if furniture of our own choosing, never before used as living utensils, proclaimed our independence and established our control over the important expectations of our life together.

"Who's Ella?" I asked.

"That's our daughter's name. Ella. Isn't she beautiful?"

"How did we name her Ella?"

"Well," she paused to indicate I should pay attention, "because Bella means beautiful. But boy begins with the letter B, and Ella is a girl, so I threw out the B and made Ella."

Our baby had a name, and she became more real to us,

like new furniture not yet delivered.

Over the next few weeks, we scoured the Sears catalogue.

First the crib. Its color and style foreshadowed the direction of our decisions. We agreed on a white frame with muted yellow, green, and orange flowers painted on the headboard. The gate slid up and down easily, according to the ad, and the spring frame adjusted so that during her early months, the mattress sat high, and we could reach her easily without straining our backs. As Ella grew, we could lower the frame to accommodate her growth.

Charlene added a matching changing table that came with an infant-sized, plastic bathtub, also white. She included a dresser, bed linens, fluffy towels, and a baby sponge.

I pointed out a rocking cradle that I thought would match, but Charlene hesitated.

"I don't want to rock my baby without holding her, Daniel. Wouldn't you prefer a rocking chair? It's more intimate."

I imagined holding that tiny life force, cuddled against me, totally trusting and loving, and I pictured that rocking chair in that corner across from Ella's crib. It seemed right.

Charlene placed the orders and arranged for deliveries. Sears gave us more credit, and all I had to do was make enough money to pay for everything. I began to feel the discomfort of debt, a queasy feeling like that of work uncompleted at the end of the day. I developed an insistent apprehension about things I could not put into words. It bothered me so much, I could not sleep.

One particularly sleepless night I went to the kitchen and made a cup of tea. I headed toward the living room to think, but instead, I walked into Ella's room. I sat down on the rocking chair, and holding the steaming cup in both hands, I pushed off the floor, easily, rhythmically. I closed my eyes, and I was holding Ella. She was snuggling against my cheek, and I was a father, a protector. I was lulled into a state of unusual clarity, deeply connected to our unborn child. I loved her already.

At some point, Charlene touched my shoulder and startled me.

"What are you doing?" she asked.

I opened my eyes and stopped rocking.

"Hey."

She came to me and took the cup and placed it on the floor.

She sat on my lap, and we rocked, each in our own solitude of expectation.

"She's going to be beautiful," Charlene said.

"Yes. Like you."

She smiled. "Let's go to bed."

I slept well that night, but in the morning, instead of studying, I worried again about finances.

I called Mark. We met at the pool hall and ordered a

beer.

"Have you thought about what you'll do for money?" Mark asked. "You're having a kid."

"I know. I know. All the time. Food. Clothes. College. Insurance. A house. I don't know how I'll do it."

"You need a full time job. I can get you on selling cars."

"Thanks, Mark, I appreciate the offer. I just can't see myself there."

"I guess you could go full time at the Bistro."

"That's what I've been thinking, but Charlene has this thing about Ronaldo. She wants me to quit."

"No can do," he admonished. "You've got bills. I've been trying to tell you. That school thing is a sham. Get out into the world. Make some real money."

Mark's advice made sense. The truth is, I not only wanted this baby, I wanted others. I thought I might finish college first and settle into a secure business career, but one cannot always control circumstances, and sometimes, opportunity springs forth amid difficulties. I decided against Charlene's bias against Ronaldo, and instead, I leaned on Mark's work experiences and on his suggestion. I asked Ronaldo for help.

That evening, I arrived at work half an hour early. I caught Ronaldo's attention and motioned toward the office, gesturing that I wanted to talk. He maintained the restaurant office on the second level overlooking the dining area. I figured that Patricia chose the furnishings because the long, polished desk and stuffed chair looked like her doing; so too, the lighting, and the art pieces.

I stood near the desk.

"Have a seat," he said.

I looked at the chair. It seemed a mile away.

"No thanks. I only need a minute."

"What's so important you can't sit down?"

"I need to work full time."

"I don't have anything full time right now, Daniel."

"Ronaldo, I've been with you almost three years. Isn't there anything?"

"If I had something, I would."

Business negotiations were new to me, and I wasn't sure how to proceed. I lit a cigarette.

"We're broke," I said. "Charlene bought new furniture. The baby's coming."

I didn't know what else to say.

"What about school?"

"I've got to work, Ronaldo. I'm quitting school. If you don't have anything, I'll have to go full time somewhere."

He leaned back in the chair. He didn't say anything, just kept looking at me, as if he were measuring me for a suit. I felt uncomfortable. The cigarette distracted me, and I put it out in the ashtray.

"What is it?" I asked.

"Sit down," he said.

I sat.

"I've been thinking about opening another place. Nothing fancy. A small bar, neighborhood kind of place. Booze and finger food. Maybe a pool table."

I nodded.

"Something for the college kids, you know?"

"That's great, Ronaldo. Will you have something full time there?"

"How would you like to run it?"

"Run it?"

"Own it, really. Sort of like partners. You do all the work, and I take some of the profit."

"You're joking, right?"

"Not at all," he said. "I've been toying with the idea for more than a year. Didn't know quite how to pull it off because I didn't have anyone I could trust to run it. It'll be good for both of us. Give you something to do full time. Make me a couple of bucks, too. Let me get with the accountant and the attorney. Meantime, I'll get you a few more hours here. Now you go tell that pretty wife of yours not to worry."

"Ronaldo, this is great," I said. "Really. Thanks. You won't regret it."

Chapter 16

The great dreams of ordinary lives, in their simplicity, distract from tragedy. Not even a Magi could have foreseen the ripples of my decision to quit school and go into business with Ronaldo.

I called Mark and set up lunch. We met at the Depot Diner, down the street from the car lot, a converted railroad car with silver siding. He liked to sit in the corner booth at the end of the car. The waitress brought coffee. Mark ordered an egg salad sandwich and winked at her. I ordered tuna salad.

"The irony worries me," I said. "It's no shame being poor. I accept that. But the stress of not having money for our needs feels greater than the needs themselves."

"You're thinking too much. Never look a gift horse in the mouth. Take his offer. It's what you want."

"That's just it. We have no money. I haven't finished school. And I don't know how to run a business."

"Haven't I been telling you there's no money in school? What are you getting out of it, except debt? You've been studying business long enough, and you've learned enough from books. You want your own business, and if a guy like Ronaldo thinks enough of you to front you a bar, what are you afraid of?"

"I'm not afraid, Mark. Really. I'm just a little cautious."

"Caution is fear. Listen, this is a one time opportunity,

and you're gonna love having coin in your pocket. In fact, you can start enjoying that feeling by buying lunch. You owe me some."

"Yeah."

The waitress brought more coffee. Mark stirred in his three spoonsful of sugar.

"I've got a great idea," he said. "There's a nice little red Camaro on the lot. Low miles. A real looker. You need a set of wheels if you're going to look like a successful business-man. You know, look the part to feel the part. Fake it till you make it."

"Oh, no. I haven't even started yet. I'm already in debt. I can't afford a car."

"No problem. I can set up a payment plan. I'm sure my boss will carry you a few months until you get the bar going."

"I don't know."

"I do know. It won't be a problem. We move some front payments to the end of the contract and add a little extra interest. I'll take care of it. Let's go."

We drove to the Buy Here Pay Here Auto Dealership, Mark in his ten year old Alpha Romeo that looked new and shiny, me in my old Ford that looked old and dingy.

The red Camaro stood out from the sedans like a strobe light in a church. The sun glistened along the contour of the body, highlighting bright spots and emphasizing thin black shadows at the creases of the hood and the doors. The detailer had sprayed rubber shine on the tires, and even the wheels looked sexy.

"Whoa, Mark. That's not me."

"Of course it's you, and you know it. I'll get the keys."

I touched the door handle. The sporty arrogance suggested a kind of reckless strength that every young Californian feels born to, a rock n' roll, billboard bright, real American muscle dream. I was suddenly half James Dean, half Elvis Presley, and half J. P. Morgan.

At that moment, I knew I could not buy the car.

Mark returned with the keys.

"I can't buy this car, Mark. Charlene wouldn't approve."

"What does Charlene have to do with this?" He jangled the keys. "It's just your head getting in the way. Charlene will love it."

"No, she won't. And you know it. But you're right about us needing a car. A family car. Something safe. Something, you know, for a family."

I could see the conflicting mechanisms of his brain struggle to satisfy his salesman's need to sell something and his friendship's concern that the something be reasonable.

He tapped his temple with a long, bony finger.

"Follow me."

We walked toward the back area of the lot to a square masonry block building with two bays, one with a lift for mechanical work, the other a car wash and polish area.

"It's not quite ready. Needs a couple of tires and some

spit shine, but it's a real steal."

He pointed to a light beige station wagon with plastic wood side trim, four doors, and a third seat that folded down to make storage space.

"Best family car we've had in a long time. Only five years old, low miles, sturdy as a tank, and a great looker. What do you think?"

"It's fantastic," I said. "Do you think I can really afford something like that?"

"Let me talk to the boss. I'll see what I can do. But if I pull this off, you owe me."

"Right," I said.

I walked to the car.

"Does it need much work?" I asked the mechanic.

"Tires. That's all. This one's really clean. We don't get many like it."

I nodded. I wanted it. I knew Charlene would approve. I could already see the kids climbing across the seats, arguing who would get to sit in back, who would get the window.

Mark returned.

"Sorry, buddy," he frowned. "She's too expensive for you." Then he laughed. "Just kidding. I talked the old man into giving you seven hundred and fifty for that junker you've got. Believe me, no one else would give you more than five hundred. That will swing the deal."

"You can do it? Really?"

"Why don't we take her for a spin? See if you like it.

You can show me the bar."

"All right," I said. "Let's."

I drove off the lot across town to the strip mall where Ronaldo had rented a space for the new bar.

"There in the corner," I pointed. "They're installing the bar and the stools next week. Then the detail stuff, two TV sets, tables and chairs, booths, all that. It should be ready to open by the end of December, and I'll be up and running by the first of the year."

"Kick ass," Mark said. "Let's get the paperwork finished so you can take this baby home and show it to Charlene."

The paper work took an hour.

"Nothing down. Thirteen and a half percent. Thirty-six months. No payments for three months. Balloon payment at the end. Sign here."

"I didn't realize the payments would be so high."

"Buyer's remorse. Don't worry. With all the money you'll be making at the bar, after you make a couple of regular car payments, you won't even think about it. Remember, that two thousand a month Ronaldo is paying you is just an advance against profits. Every quarter, you'll get a fat bonus, and you'll be making so much money you won't know what to do with them."

I looked at him.

"And, I'll be your biggest customer." He smiled. "Sign here."

I signed.

Adventure in life, it seemed to me, must occur outside the confines of ordinary days, and I felt extraordinary, and, I admit, destined for adventure. The buyer's remorse uncertainty floated out of my mind and out the window into the wind as I drove home. I honked the horn as I pulled into the driveway. Charlene walked out to the porch.

"What do you think?" I called, my arm resting on the door panel, my smile as resplendent as the liquid rubber shine on the tires.

"Daniel," she said

She walked down the steps to the passenger door.

"Hop in," I said, but she had already closed the door.

"What's going on?"

"I bought it from Mark. He made me a great deal. Do you like it?"

"What's not to like?"

"It's an early Christmas present."

We drove out toward the foothills and into the lazy afternoon.

"Charlene, our luck is changing."

Chapter 17

As Charlene and I grew into that closeness the progress of pregnancy brings to two people, subtle changes in Mark and Odette's relationship began. For example, Odette spent much time at our house. She and Charlene discussed housekeeping, furniture, dishes, babies, and love. Odette said she was falling in love with Mark, and Charlene assured her that could only lead to marriage.

Odette did not quit her job at The Bistro, but between her work and her visits with Charlene, her time with Mark became more and more important to her. Mark, on the other hand, began working longer evenings and more Saturdays because those are the times when used car buyers are most likely to buy.

One afternoon, Odette stopped by the house before work. We sat in the living room. Odette's eyes sparkled, and they seemed to absorb her surroundings rather than to see them. She remained quiet.

Charlene lit a cigarette and smiled at me from behind the smoke.

"If you don't tell me what's going on," she said to Odette, "I'll explode."

Odette smiled.

"I'm in love."

"This is not news," Charlene said.

"Mark has been really busy the last couple of months.

But he's been making lots of sales, and last night he brought me roses and a bracelet made from pearls."

She extended her arm for us to see.

Charlene pulled her legs up under her.

"More."

"He asked me to forgive him for working so hard. I think he's getting ready to propose."

"Really?"

"Well, he's working longer hours. Making more money. Bringing me sweet gifts. He must be getting ready to ask. He's just getting enough money together maybe to buy us a house."

Charlene jumped from the couch and hugged Odette, both of them smiling and nodding their heads. I'm not convinced they remembered I was in the room.

"When do you think he'll ask?" Charlene wanted to know.

"You know Mark. But I have an idea."

"Tell."

"Let's plan a weekend at the ski lodge. It'll be a reward for his hard work, and we can be alone in a romantic place. It will make it easy for him. He'll ask me then."

"Yes," Charlene agreed. "Just the two of you."

"No, all of us," Odette insisted.

Charlene's face darkened slightly, and she lost enough enthusiasm that I noticed. I figured she wanted them to be alone. Odette seemed to miss the change in Charlene's attitude, and she continued.

"We can go late Saturday afternoon. He won't want to miss his best sales day."

The plans began.

"Daniel," Odette continued, "you must keep this a secret from Mark. You can drive up after us. In your new car. He'll be so surprised."

"Okay," I said. "I'll leave the details to you two. I have to get to work."

I kissed Charlene. "I love you," I said. "I'll see you later, Odette."

The foundations of agreement when women plan ensue from trust, a condition of equanimity missing in the business of men. The focus of womanhood upon maternity and familial bonds exists within the spirit, not on paper. It is a shared familiarity as profound as the cycles of the moon, and as enduring. Such elegant faith produces earthly joy unknown in the world of commerce. The propriety of generational continuity trumps every court of law. When such plans go astray, however, the world is wounded.

I did not at first comprehend the importance of such trust in the future. Doctor Leonard expressed opposition to this thinking, comparing it to witchcraft and prophetic charlatanry.

I'm not so sure.

Two weekends later, we drove to Donner through afternoon sunlight into a dense forest of pungent air and cool shade. Unpolluted mountains fulfill a mysterious, genetically coded invitation to return to ancestral knowledge of beasts and prophesy. We arrived at the lodge as evening began. The light snow of mid-November portended a profitable coming ski season, and the chill of late autumn mountain air invigorated us like the news of childbirth.

Mark was indeed surprised to see us. When we pulled into the secluded parking area behind them, he raised his eyebrows. He said nothing, but I think he suspected collusion.

The women wanted to freshen up and change before eating, so Mark and I walked to the bar.

Denny greeted us like old friends.

"First one's on me," he said. "Welcome."

"Two scotches, and keep them coming," Mark ordered.

Two other tables had guests, three at one, two at the other, but the room felt quiet and comfortable. The view out the great windows displayed the trails and motionless chairlifts in transient shadow. The blue-green needles of the stern Sierra cedars turned gray with dark shadows as the evening collapsed toward twilight.

"To your big weekend," I toasted.

"My big weekend?"

Mark put his glass on the table. "Okay, Daniel, what gives?"

"You don't know?" I teased.

Mark leaned back in the chair and assumed his salesman smile with eyes that look right at you but which only see your wallet. He eased a pack of cigarettes from his pocket, pulled one out, struck a match, and raised the flame slowly, all the while looking at me with both eyes. He fanned out the match, exhaled up into the turbulence of the ceiling fan, and circled his finger toward Denny, indicating another round. He lifted his glass. Still watching me, he downed the scotch.

Denny brought two fresh glasses.

"Okay," Mark said. "I give. What's up?"

Thinking he was pulling my leg, I went directly to the matter.

"Did you bring the ring?"

"What ring?"

"Come on," I said. "Let me see it before they get here."

"Daniel, I don't have a ring."

"Serious?"

"Serious."

"You going to give her a ring later?"

"What are you talking about?"

"Odette," I said, half a statement, half a question.

"Odette wants to get pregnant," he said, by way of interpretation.

"Like Charlene?"

"Yes. Just like Charlene."

He lifted his glass in salute to insinuate I had finally

gotten something right and sipped his drink.

"Maybe you better explain," I said. "I don't think I'm caught up."

"Daniel, I cannot get pregnant right now. I'm not ready. Besides, Odette thinks if she gets pregnant, I'll marry her."

"Odette thinks you're going to propose this weekend."

"Where'd she get an idea like that?"

"You haven't been spending much time with her lately."

"So?"

"She thinks you're working extra to save money for a house."

He looked up to the ceiling and exhaled smoke into the whirling fan blades. He motioned with his finger for another round.

"Truth is, I wanted to talk to you about a new friend I met a couple of weeks ago. Her name's Vivian. A real looker. Class, you know? More my style than Odette. I don't have any plans to marry Odette, Danny boy, but let's not tell her that just yet."

"What are you saying, Mark? You're not going to marry Odette? In fact, you're seeing another woman?"

"I don't want to stop seeing Odette. I just want a little more excitement."

"I'm not sure what to say, Mark."

"You've got to talk to Charlene. Have her tell Odette how awful pregnancy is. Morning sickness, gaining weight, stuff like that, so she'll drop this having a baby thing."

"I don't know. Charlene's pretty excited about our baby."

"You've got to try."

"I can't promise that, Mark. This is way outside the plan."

"I knew I could count on you."

When the girls arrived, Mark behaved as if our conversation had not happened. Throughout the meal, Charlene and Odette traded knowing glances, and dinner finished without incident.

On the walk back to our room, the steak I ate gave me heartburn. I had to tell Charlene. But how?

Chapter 18

We walked to the bungalow along a path lined with red fir trees, one hundred feet tall, magical and mysterious, as if at any moment we might meet an elf spirit of the forest. The cold mountain air smelled dense with the aroma of sweet decay in undergrowth mulch and the tangy startle of pine pitch. The night sky, free of artificial globes, opened the heavens to so many stars we couldn't count them.

"It's beautiful here," I said.

"It's dangerous," Charlene said.

I smiled. The dense forests, the stark cleanliness of the air, the sky so close you could touch it, all harbingers of possible, hidden dangers within nature perhaps, but beautiful nonetheless.

On the way into the room, I brought two logs from the pile on the porch. I placed one log on the grate and made a fire. I could not delay confiding to Charlene, and as we sat on the sofa, we watched flames of orange and yellow rise and fall within the split sides of the burning logs.

"Did you enjoy our meal?" I asked.

"The food was fine," she said. "But Mark was holding back."

"What do you mean?"

"Something about his shoulders," she said. "They didn't seem truthful. Did you notice?"

"I didn't notice anything about his shoulders," I

admitted.

She pulled my arm close to her and held it.

"He's leaving Odette, isn't he?" she said.

"Leaving her? Why would you say that?"

"She's pregnant, and he doesn't want the baby."

"She's pregnant?"

"Didn't he tell you?"

"He doesn't know. He thinks she wants to get pregnant."

"She's already pregnant. It's a bad omen."

"What kind of talk is that?"

"I told you never to bring us to this place again."

"Charlene, you and Odette decided to come here."

"The spirits of those who were eaten are all around us, and they're angry."

"Charlene, you're talking nonsense."

"Listen. You can hear them."

"Hear who?"

"The ghosts."

"You hear ghosts?"

"Listen."

The mesmerizing glow from the fire lit and dimmed the pine paneled walls with the erratic dance of flame burst. The crackling of the spent wood pierced the eerie quiet.

She pulled away from me and sat straight with her back against the cushion. She did not look at me.

"We invited danger coming here," she said.

In the gloom of the moment, a sudden crash outside the door startled me, and I jumped.

"They're here," Charlene said. "Outside, by the wood pile, against the door."

"Who?"

"The wolves."

"Wolves?"

I jumped from the couch and ran to the door. I secured the lock and stepped quietly to the side of the window. I looked out into the silence of the strange darkness. With the forms of trees and bushes highlighted by the cold light of the alpine moon, nature seemed suddenly fearsome.

"I don't see anything," I whispered.

"It's a white wolf. He carries the angry spirits of the dead from the Donner party. They don't want us here."

Her attitude and her words made me jittery. Her eyes turned opaque and intense at the same time, as if she could see through the walls and pierce the secrets of the black forest night.

"I don't think there's anything out there," I said. "You're just upset about Odette."

I eased the door open. I looked across the small porch. I saw nothing. I opened the door a little more. Without leaving the room, I looked into the night, a blank mystery of uncertainty. Wind rustled the high reaches of the trees, and the branches undulated, disrupting the silence in the same way a squeaking rocker disturbs contemplation.

"It's the wind," I said.

I could not see into the blackest shade of the forest, could ascertain no concrete image except what my imagination conjured. I stepped onto the porch, holding the doorknob with one hand, leaving the door open and the safety of the room accessible. A log had fallen from the wood pile. It lay alone, alongside the kindling chips. Except for a continuous whisper of the high wind, no other sound disturbed the stillness. I returned to the room, locked the door, and sat again next to Charlene.

"A piece of wood fell."

"What caused it, Daniel? He knocked it down so you will believe. They are gathering. We must leave."

"Leave?"

"Yes. We must not listen to their complaints or we will suffer, and a baby will die."

"But, Charlene, it's late. What about Mark and Odette? And what do you mean a baby will die?"

"They have a car, and they know about Mark."

"Who knows what?"

"Stop, Daniel. We must leave."

She grimaced, and her eyes looked farther away. She pushed her hands against her stomach as if in pain.

"What is it?"

"Please, Daniel. I can't protect you much longer. We must leave now."

"All right," I said. "We'll go."

Chapter 19

When I had a chance to explain our late night departure to Mark, he said, "Charlene is acting weird. You best get her some help."

I did not, of course, get her help since I interpreted his comment as sarcasm rather than prescription. Much later, when I described Charlene's unusual reaction at Donner Pass to Doctor Leonard, he explained that wolves have long held prominence in mythological tradition and that Charlene had most likely absorbed an ancient archetype of mothering. I contended that a log fell from the firewood stack and Charlene is a sensitive woman, prone to deep emotions, and those emotions were exacerbated due to the hormonal excesses of pregnancy.

Doctor Leonard suggested that my life might prove more comfortable if I submitted willingly to his wisdom.

"All wisdom," I told him, "is subject to one's point of view."

To that, he relit his pipe.

Chapter 20

The construction of the bar began to take final shape. I met Ronaldo at his accountant's office on Monday. His attorney and his accountant waited.

When I walked in, Ronaldo greeted me.

"You ready to become the next California millionaire?"

"Sure am," I said.

"John Pallagrini. I'm Mr. Geordano's attorney."

We shook hands.

"Alexander Wilshire. Accountant."

"Nice to meet you."

They all smiled and made me feel like one of them. We sat around a rectangular wood table, polished to a high shine with no fingerprints showing.

"Shall we get started?" Ronaldo said.

The attorney passed a copy of the contract to Ronaldo and a copy to me. He sat on my right. He flipped several pages and stopped on page four.

"Sign here first. There by the X. Ronaldo, you sign on the line below."

Before I finished my signature, I noticed $1,000 in one of the paragraphs.

"What's that thousand dollars refer to?" I asked.

"That's your advance against profits," Mr. Pallagrini said.

"Ronaldo, you told me that my advance would be two

thousand."

"I did, Daniel, but construction costs ran over budget because I put the contractor on overtime. I did that for you."

"For me?"

"Yes. I knew you needed to get working full time. Any delay would cost you money."

That second thousand dollars meant a lot to us. We never had extra money, and without my student loans, I wasn't sure a thousand guarantee would cover our needs. Charlene was already upset with me for doing business with Ronaldo, and this would surely add to her displeasure.

"I can't do it," I said. "We need a stable income, and a thousand a month isn't enough."

"But Daniel," Ronaldo reasoned, "you are forgetting your tips. You will easily make a thousand a month tending the bar. And," he paused, "and, you don't have to claim tips. It's like free money. Certainly, Charlene kept a few dollars from Uncle Sam."

The fact is, Charlene did not keep anything of the sort. She was honest in all matters. Still, what would I do about an income? I quit school. I didn't have another lead on a job. I bought a car.

The economics of uncertainty filled my head, and at that moment, I forgot everything I ever learned in school. Although accountants and attorneys are the two driving forces of business profit, I did not feel safe sitting with an accountant on one side of me and an attorney on the other. I imagined them exhaling from flared nostrils, as if their smoldering silence implicated my youth and my inexperience.

Ronaldo gestured to the paper.

I signed.

The attorney flipped to the next signature area at the bottom of a page full of numbers. I paused again and looked at the accountant.

"A breakdown of the start-up costs, and a repayment schedule," Mr. Wilshire explained.

I'd studied and manipulated lots of numbers in my business classes, all of which were practice for a grade. But each one of these numbers affected me personally, my family, and my future.

"It cost one hundred and twenty thousand dollars to get the tenant improvements made?"

"I told you the labor costs ran over," Ronaldo answered. "Besides, this figure includes the TV, pots, and pans, glasses, and so on. And the first three month's lease."

I looked at him.

"You won't let me down, will you, Daniel? I've put my confidence in you. It's time to show me I haven't made a mistake."

"No. No," I insisted. "I'm grateful, really. It's just, these numbers are so big."

"Only because you don't know the gross a business like

this can generate. Besides, Mr. Wilshire will manage the books for us. Taxes, pay the bills, the lease, payroll. And to really get you started as a businessman, I instructed him and Mr. Pallagrini to arrange for financing the costs as a business loan in your name. That's a real advantage to you, being young and just getting started."

"In my name?"

"Yes. You're going to own it all eventually, and with the loan already in your name, the changeover will be easy. Really both of us are paying the loan. From the business, of course. But you're getting all the credit."

"Ronaldo, how can I do all this?"

"Same way I do. Lots of hard work. And," he looked directly at me, "I'll be looking out for you."

I nodded. I could work hard. I knew that about myself. Ronaldo was a successful businessman. I had as good a chance as anyone. I signed the rest of the contract which included my 50% share of all profits, paid quarterly, and a buy-out clause that allowed me to buy the business in five years with the proviso that Ronaldo would maintain 100% control of the name, titles, and assigns until the buy-out was completed, a clause which the attorney assured me was standard in such cases as ours.

Chapter 21

The rest of the week I spent at Whispers. Ronaldo came up with the name. He thought the college crowd would identify with the sexual innuendo. He hired a short order cook named Benny. Although he was skinny, he sported an impressive image of a man with a lion's head and alligator feet tattooed on his right forearm.

"That's my dad," he explained. "Feet on the ground, head in the air."

I nodded.

"Ronaldo said I would work Thursday through Monday from 6:00 to midnight. Those will be your busiest nights, and I'll be around for the Monday night football crowd."

"Okay," I said.

"I do my own prep and clean my cooking area," he continued. "You do the dishes."

"I guess Ronaldo told you I'm an experienced dishwasher."

He shrugged and lit a cigarette.

"I've ordered the oil, food, and condiments. They'll be here tomorrow morning. I'll come by in the afternoon and get everything ready."

On Thursday the Pinball Concession showed up. They placed a juke box in one corner, an electronic shooting game against the far wall, and a Mission To The Center Of The Other Kingdome game next to that.

On their way out, the older of the two delivery men told me, "Fifty percent for us, fifty percent for you. We collect the cash once a week. Your share goes to Mr. Wilshire's office. Here's our card. We do the maintenance if there's a problem."

Before I finished reading the card, they were gone.

I put the card in a desk drawer in the back office area, and when I returned, I discovered a young woman standing near the front door, looking around as if she might have an interest in buying the place. She had long bleached-blonde hair, fiery red lipstick, and sparkling blue eye shadow. She wore a low cut, white tee shirt with spaghetti straps, and very tight black leather shorts. The red color of her sneakers matched her red belt.

"I'm sorry, Miss. We're not open yet."

"I'm Tina. I give ten percent of my tips to the cook and ten percent to the dishwasher, fifteen percent if he helps me bus the tables. I keep the rest."

"I'm not sure I get your point."

"Ronaldo hired me. I start Sunday. I'm off Tuesdays and Wednesdays."

"Ronaldo hired you?"

"You must be Daniel. He said you were real quick on the uptake."

"I'm also the owner. You might want to keep that in mind."

She looked me over and nodded her head slowly.

"Okay," she said. "I'll see you Sunday."

I admit, she made a tantalizing vision as she walked away.

I sat on the end bar stool. Benny and Tina seemed experienced hands, but they didn't fit the profiles of employees at The Bistro. I wondered where Ronaldo knew these people from. I also wondered how much influence he thought his fifty percent granted him. I decided to close things down for the day. I locked the back area and turned off the lights. As I prepared to turn off the lights in the bar area, the front door opened, and a tall man in his early thirties pushed the front door open. He smiled in such a friendly way I felt like I already knew him. He waved and called out, "Hey, Daniel. I'm Bob. You know, Bob from Brooklyn. Remember me?"

His Jimi Hendrix tee shirt fit tight around his torso, and it was probably an extra large. He looked like a weight lifter.

"I'm not sure I remember you, Bob," I admitted.

"We've never been introduced," he said. "But I've seen you at The Bistro. I deliver Ronaldo's beer."

"Oh, yeah. No wonder you look familiar."

"Listen," he said, "I need a few hours to get you set up. Sorry about the suddenness, but you know Ronaldo, always last minute."

I raised my eyebrows.

"Anyhow, if you're okay with it, I'll be here about two o'clock tomorrow afternoon to set up your taps, hang the neons, get things in order. Then on Saturday, I'll fill the coolers so you can open on Sunday for the football crowd. After that, I'll make regular deliveries on Fridays, so you'll be set for the weekend and for the following week. I work on Saturday mornings. I keep those hours for emergencies."

"Sure," I said. "That all sounds fine. I'll see you tomorrow."

"Good. See you then."

He patted my back like we were old friends. Then he left.

I turned off the lights. As I locked the front door, I spoke out loud, "Welcome to the real world, Danny boy."

As inappropriate as it might seem, I answered myself.

"Yes," I said. "Welcome."

Chapter 22

Ambition overcomes fear through recklessness, and it pacifies reason with idealized expectation. Momentary setbacks wither in the heat of desire, and reality's sharp edges blur to indistinguishable wrinkles outside the intense focus of a determined work ethic. That night, as I pocketed the key, I admired the subtle elegance of our sign, the word *Whispers* in red neon and the single-line silhouette of a female face whispering into the ear of an attentive male. As I looked, I recognized that I had managed the first step of the entrepreneurial elite, my own business. So many images of success flashed in and out of my imagination that by the time I arrived home I had a new house, two cars, the adoration of women, the respect of men, and the indulgent power of wealth. When I parked, I hardly recognized our house, I had wandered mentally so far from it.

Charlene did not greet me at the door. Instead, I found her, sitting on the couch, smoking a cigarette, sipping a cup of tea, and deep in conversation with Odette. Odette sat at the other end of the couch, she also with a cup of tea, its steam creeping gently along the roll of her cheek. Charlene had entered her second trimester, and she sat in the corner of the couch, comfortable and at ease. Her stomach rounded out, but otherwise her lovely body looked the same, her legs stretched comfortably, her feet resting on the cushion. Odette seemed more tense. Her gaze across the top of the cup penetrated the steam and focused on my entrance. Her own pregnancy had not yet begun to show, but somehow her body language displayed the fact that she carried a child.

"Hi," I said.

I walked to Charlene. She did not turn her head to receive my kiss. I kissed her cheek. Odette's stare remained steady.

I sat in the chair.

"What's going on?"

Neither woman spoke.

"Sunday's our big day," I ventured.

"You're not going to open that business, are you?" Odette said.

"Of course I am."

"Even though Ronaldo cut your advance in half? How will you pay your bills? How can you continue to trust him?"

"Odette, you've worked for him longer than I have. You know him. Why wouldn't I trust him?"

Charlene held a quiet, soft, maternal patience upon her face.

"Charlene," I pleaded, "I thought we had discussed all this, and you were fine with the arrangements. Don't you have anything to say to Odette?"

"I have much to say to Odette. I have nothing to say to you. In fact, I'm not talking to you."

The surprise I felt at hearing these words measured in equivalency to that which I might feel if I awoke one morning to discover I had two noses. The confidence and excitement that filled me during the drive home dissipated.

"What is it?" I asked.

Odette answered. "It's not enough money to pay your monthly bills. You have a child coming. You must get a real job."

"Owning a business is a real job. In fact, it's more than a real job. All those hours, the extra responsibilities."

"Exactly," Odette interrupted. "Why do you want to be away from your wife all that time? At night? In a bar?"

"That's enough, Charlene," I said, ignoring Odette. "It's done. The bar opens on Sunday."

Charlene sipped her tea, her placid countenance like the look of a Madonna entranced by an angelic announcement.

"Well?" I waited.

"You have upset the flavor of my tea," she said. "Odette, I must retire to my room. Please inform Daniel that the couch will arrive between 9:00 and 10:00 tomorrow morning, and he must remove this old couch before then."

"What couch?" I asked.

"Good evening, Odette," Charlene said, and she removed herself to our bedroom.

Odette rose and placed her tea cup on the small side table.

"We bought a couch today. Christmas is coming, you

know. How could you let your wife continue to sit on this old thing in her condition? I thought more of you, Daniel. Bring this old one to Goodwill. If they'll even take it."

"We bought a couch today? You bought a couch today?"

Odette reached the door. She turned as she prepared to leave, but before she could speak, Charlene re-entered the room.

"Daniel," she said, "in Arctic tribes, children may be considered twins if they are born to two sisters at the same time. Odette's child and mine will be twin sisters."

She looked at Odette, and they both smiled.

"Did you know," Charlene continued, "that the predominant road kill in Louisiana is armadillo? The armadillo's startle response includes jumping into the air before forming itself into a protective ball. When it is frightened by an oncoming car, it jumps into the air at exactly the height of a car's front bumper. One must learn to understand one's own startle response."

Then, with a firm sense of completion, she exited down the hallway.

Odette nodded knowingly and pulled the door closed behind her.

Chapter 23

I learned a few things my first weeks in business. For one thing, Ronaldo knew what he was doing hiring Benny and Tina. Benny turned out to be punctual, reasonably tidy, a fair maker of burgers and sandwiches, and he never missed a day of work in the three months he worked for me. Tina, too, knew her way around. Her sexy dress and come-on demeanor brought boys to the bar like a night light beckons moths. With boys in the bar, girls showed up, and we stayed pretty steady almost from the first night. She tolerated the flirtations, invited some, and she had a way of turning almost every remark into a drink order.

Ronaldo expected the bar to open every day. I worked the first two weeks with no day off. Added to that, I took no time off during the three weeks of prep work prior to opening. Nearly 40 days without a day off. The excitement of a new business compelled participation. Nevertheless, by the third week, I had enough of a seven-day work week, and I made a corporate decision to close the bar on Tuesdays. Fortunately, Ronaldo said nothing. In fact, I saw less of him than I saw of Charlene. Truth is, I saw more of Mark than anyone else.

That's another thing I learned. When Mark promised to become my best customer, he meant it. He showed up almost every night after they closed shop, usually eight o'clock or so, and the first thing he attempted was to get a date with Tina.

"She's working," I said. "Leave her alone."

"She's a real looker."

"Doesn't matter," I told him. "Besides, you're supposed to be dating Odette."

That subject became something of a non-subject, however. Although Odette remained committed to Mark, envisioning a small cottage, a white picket fence, and happily ever after, Mark had neither the desire nor the intention of sanctioning her hopes. He still did not know she was pregnant.

He liked to sit at the end of the bar where the short portion of the "L" met the wall. He sat on the stool and observed. Sometimes he would stand, one foot resting on the boot rail, his gangly arms stretched along the top of the bar. If things slowed a little, I would walk over so we could talk.

"That one with the red top," he might say. Or, "That one in the tight blue jeans," by way of advising me which girl he would court that night. He liked to take his money-clip from his pocket to pay for their drinks. His slow, exaggerated gestures emphasized the wealth within his reach, and some women found delight in measuring him against the college boys who did not own a money-clip.

One Monday evening, he arrived late. He strode to his seat.

"Regular?" I asked him.

He tapped the bar-top with his finger.

I brought him a beer and a cold glass.

"What's up?"

He leaned across the bar and whispered.

"Just finished a two car deal. Mom and dad stopped by to find a car for their little darling who is headed off to school. I sold her the Camaro, and I sold them my Alpha. I'm fat, baby."

He pushed away from the bar, sat up straight, and looked up toward the ceiling. I suspected he was counting the dollars of his night's work.

"I'm happy for you," I said.

He lifted the bottle and began to pour.

"Get yourself one. On me. We're celebrating."

I drew a draft, and we touched glasses. Several people at the other end of the bar caught my attention. We weren't too busy, so I motioned for Tina to come behind the bar and give me a few minutes.

"Now that's good," Mark said after a healthy swallow.

I agreed, taking a healthy slug of my own. That's another fact I was learning. Working at a bar provides excellent and varied opportunities to drink, opportunities that other professions cannot always offer.

"So how are you doing, Danny boy? Things look like they're good."

"I think the business is doing okay," I said. "We haven't had an accounting yet, but we're selling a lot of beer."

I pondered the glass.

"Why so gloomy then?" Mark asked.

"Nothing. We'll be okay."

"Nothing tells me something. What is it?"

"I don't get paid until the first. We haven't had any money coming in since I started. Tips haven't been great. You know. These are college kids. They don't have a lot. I've been taking some of the food from here, but Charlene hasn't been eating well. She's still upset about my partnering with Ronaldo. And all the hours . . ."

I paused, raised the glass, and said, "Same old, same old. Different day. We'll be fine."

He nodded. I nodded. We finished our beer.

"Okay," Mark said. "I'm beat. Long day." He put a twenty dollar bill on the bar. "I'll catch you," he said.

I closed that night, tired and alone. The next day, Tuesday, offered the possibility of rest, a day off. I needed it, too. No matter how much I loved working, the body needs to recuperate. And, yet, the prospect concerned me. What would happen to the bar if it closed for one day every week?

This, of course, was early in the business, and I suffered from normal start-up anxieties, perhaps complicated by a shortage of money. I drove home and fell asleep on our new couch without waking Charlene. I made every effort not to disturb her when I came home. My hours were so different from those we had grown accustomed to. And it seemed like I was always busy. The business was important, very important to us, to our future, to our baby's future. I had to get things right, learn the tricks, put in my time. It's how business works, and I didn't want to burden her with all of it. I wanted her to be comfortable, secure. I wanted to take care of her.

That's why I did what I did. I wasn't ignoring her. I was protecting her.

She didn't see things the same way.

I awoke around 10:00 the next morning. Charlene made coffee, and I fixed a cup. We sat at the kitchen table.

"You're home," she said.

Then she went silent.

Marriage creates unexpected intimacies, and their strengths or weaknesses reflect the degree and complexity of compromise that induces them. On my day at home, Charlene's silence tested me. What common experience or feeling can overcome such difficulty if not love? I searched my heart. I loved Charlene in all the ways I could conjure, and yet I felt an emotional distance between us. It felt almost physical.

"Charlene," I asked, "can we talk?"

"There's nothing to say. Why should we talk?

Thus, in response to my question, I received a question as an answer. I remained in a state of puzzlement. Puzzlement and knowledge are not necessarily related in the way, for instance, that curiosity and education might be.

If one is curious, one seeks knowledge through the pragmatic process of research and evaluation, the result of which might lead to an insight or to an educated conclusion. But puzzlement offers no such simple resolution. Puzzlement evolves from a state of peace; the puzzle occurs when one does not comprehend the cause of the consternation that perpetuated the loss of peace.

Charlene retreated to our bedroom, and I went to the living room to puzzle my puzzlement in silence.

Sometime in the late afternoon, the front doorbell rang. As I pulled the latch, Mark shouted, "Open up. We're getting worn out here."

Mark entered first, and Odette followed. Both carried stuffed bags of groceries in each arm.

"Where's Charlene?" Odette asked.

At my raised eyebrows, she nodded her understanding.

She and Mark continued to the kitchen.

"What gives?" I asked.

"Steaks and beer. Beer's out in the car. I'm driving a loaner from work. Parked behind yours. Back seat."

"What's the occasion?"

"You're kidding, right? New business. Day off. Holiday spirit. Take your pick, but get me a beer."

I carried the two six-packs from the back seat, and when I returned to the house, Odette and Mark were unpacking the bags of food, far in excess of a steak and beer celebration.

"You guys," I said.

"It's nothing," Odette said. "You'd do the same for us. Get Charlene. Tell her I have news."

I tapped gently on the bedroom door.

"Charlene?"

The room was dark, lights off, shades pulled.

She sat on the edge of the bed.

I sat next to her.

"Odette and Mark brought food."

"It's embarrassing."

"A little," I said. "It's also a kindness. An act of friendship, don't you think?"

She did not answer.

"Come on, Honey," I said, and I put an arm around her. "By the way, Odette said to tell you she has news."

She looked up into my eyes, deep into that secret area that sometimes two people share and no one else knows.

"Oh, Daniel, what's happening to me?" She put her head in my chest and cried. After a bit, she stopped. "Sometimes I don't understand anything," she whispered.

"It's scary, I know. But it's also wonderful. You're having a baby. We'll be okay," I assured her.

That night we ate steak and drank beer.

"Daniel, my boy, and Charlene," Mark said, "I want to propose a toast. To Odette and our baby."

"Odette," we chimed, and Charlene and Odette hugged, sharing something only two simultaneously pregnant women can share, something ancient and perpetual, something akin to friendship melded to propagation. To life.

Through the passage of food and talk, we shared our friendships without pretenses. A rare moment, indeed. I regret to report I have shared few since.

Chapter 24

I did not see Mark again until Friday night. He came into Whispers around 9:30 with a black-haired woman. They walked to his corner. He sat on the stool near the wall, she next to him.

"Barkeep," he called. "Two of your best. Chop-chop."

We had a fairly good crowd, and I finished getting Tina's order before I brought two beers.

"Your champagne, sir," I said, and placed the beers on the bar. "Did you desire glasses, or shall you swig directly from the source?"

"Daniel, my boy, this is Vivian. She's a real lady."

Mark raised his bottle. Vivian raised hers. They nodded to one another and drank, Vivian holding her pinky out and away from the bottle. Vivian had unusually dark eyes as impenetrable as ebony and long black eyelashes. She had a medium sized, pointed nose and soft subtle cheekbones like an adolescent maiden before coming of age. She parted her hair down the center of her head, and it hung straight and so black it reflected purple and blue, depending on how the light struck. She was thin, but not angular; womanly in a sort of experienced way, but not feminine. She preened unceasingly.

Mark drained his beer.

"An excellent year, sir. Another of equal eminence and one for the tavern-keep." He turned to Vivian. "Another, my dear?"

"No," she said. "You two have one. I'm going to powder my nose."

"Always the lady," Mark said as she left.

I brought two more. We tapped bottles.

"Who's that?" I asked. "Where's Odette? What are you doing?"

"Whoa, Amigo. One question per beer."

"Really, Mark, what's going on?"

"She's Vivian," he said. "The one I told you about. Real class, isn't she?"

"Mark, Odette's carrying your baby."

"Yes. A miracle, as all babies are miracles."

"Not funny. Not an answer."

"Yet you know I'm not a big fan of miracles."

He took a long drink. He lit a cigarette. He exhaled slowly.

"Danny," he began, "I like Odette. And I know she and Charlene are friends. But she's not the one for me."

"How did you get to that conclusion?"

"Hear me out," he said. "Drink your beer, and hear me out. Vivian has a real job. Sells insurance. Makes good dollars. Odette doesn't want to move up. She's happy at The Bistro."

"She's happy with her baby. She wants to get married."

"I know. That's the point. I shouldn't have to tell you how expensive marriage is."

The bar was dark. He didn't see me blush.

"Anyhow, I got Odette a lead on a real job selling cosmetics at Penny's. She could make what she's earning at the Bistro, a-n-d," he emphasized and by stretching it out across the air between us. "And, she can make a bonus every month depending on sales."

"That sounds okay," I admitted.

"Right you are. But she refused to even go talk to the guy. How can I marry someone who won't better herself when an opportunity like that comes along?"

"I don't know, Mark. It might sound good to you and me, but if she doesn't like it, it's not an opportunity."

"It's not about liking anything. It's about the money."

He finished his beer.

"Another. Bring three," he said.

I brought three cold ones.

"Vivian, now she's another story," he continued. "Makes enough money that between the two of us, we could buy a house on High Street, the boulevard of movers and shakers."

"Buy a house? What are you talking about? You and Vivian? What about Odette? Are you talking about marrying Vivian?"

"To tell the truth, we have broached the subject."

"Mark," I said. But I had no other words.

Vivian returned from her nose powdering, but she did not sit down.

"You've taken enough of our time," she said to me. "It's nice to meet you, but we must run."

"The little lady has spoken," Mark said.

He slid off the stool and snatched the beer I brought for Vivian. He gestured to the other bottles.

"Put them on my bill, will you, buddy?"

"We don't carry tabs here, Mark," I said.

How on earth would I explain this to Charlene?

Chapter 25

The next morning, before I left for work, I told Charlene about Vivian and what Mark said about Odette.

"Why do you hate him?" she asked. "I thought he was your friend."

"What do you mean by that?"

"Do you know the most common road kill in New York? Deer. Do you know why? Because deer are pretty, and New Yorkers are not."

Chapter 26

At the end of the month, when I finally got paid, Charlene took the car to go shopping. We were still two months away from my first bonus check, but having some money felt good. I hoped that tips would begin to increase, too. Early in the afternoon, I received a call from a towing company that I needed to pay the towing fee to re-claim the car. I called Tina, who agreed to come in early. Mark drove me to pick up the car. He knew the owner.

"What's this all about?" I asked when we got to the counter.

"Your wife stopped the car in the middle of the intersection. She got out and walked down the street. Left the car running."

He pushed a release form across the counter.

"Sign there," he said. "Someone called the police, and they called me."

"Where's my wife?"

"Funny thing. When the cops caught up with her, they asked her why she left the car. She told them there was a dead body in the trunk."

"A dead body?"

"Yeah. She said you worked for the Mafia and you put it there."

"She did?"

"I heard them talking. They were coming to get you, but

when they opened the trunk, it was empty. They asked her where's the body, and she told them, right there. It's Jimmy Hoffa. You've been looking for him, haven't you?"

He handed me the bill.

"Hundred and twenty-five dollars," he said. "Well, you can guess they were puzzled, so they asked her to describe the body. Know what she told them?"

"What?" I asked, stunned at the hundred and twenty-five dollar fee.

"She asked them, do you know what the most common road kill is in Idaho? They asked her what? She told them potatoes. She said potatoes are not the brightest of road kill. They haven't learned how to grow legs, only eyes."

He laughed. "Potato eyes? Eyes of the potato? I thought it was funny. The cops didn't."

"I expect they didn't," I said. "What did they do?"

"Called an ambulance and sent her to the hospital. I guess she's up on the sixth floor right now."

I turned to Mark. "Charlene took my check book. Can you cover this for me?"

"What are you going to do?" he asked

"Try to find her."

"You sure?"

"Of course I'm sure."

As I turned to leave, Mark held my shoulder.

"Hold on there, Danny boy," he said. "Jimmy, can I get our regular discount for this?" He pointed at me. "Friend of mine."

"Sure thing, Mark. Any friend of yours." He eyed me suspiciously. "Seventy-five, then."

"Here you go. One more thing, Jimmy."

"What's that?"

"Where'd they take the lady?"

"Saint Mary's. Heard it on the CB." He pointed over his shoulder to the black box on the shelf.

"Here's your keys."

"Thanks, Jimmy. I'll be seeing you."

"Right."

Outside, Mark handed me the keys.

"You owe me a hundred."

I nodded. "Thanks."

"What are friends for?"

I drove to the hospital emergency room. A nurse from the psych unit led me to the elevator. On the sixth floor, she unlocked a door. We passed through that door, and she closed it. Immediately, we faced a second steel door with a wire-glass window slotted at face level. She pushed a red button and a buzzer rang. A small, girlish face appeared at the window. After she looked at us, another buzzer sounded, and that door opened slowly, mechanically. The woman who opened the door did not speak. She backed away as we passed into a long hallway.

We stopped at the second door on the right. The nurse knocked.

"Come in," we heard.

The sign on the door read, Doctor Leonard, Chief.

"Mr. Reed," the nurse said.

"Thank you. Sit with Mrs. Reed for a few minutes, will you?"

She nodded and left.

"Please, Mr. Reed, have a seat."

He motioned to two chairs in front of his desk. I sat in the one closest to the wall.

"Now," Doctor Leonard said, "what can I do for you?"

"You can tell me what's going on."

"How do you mean?"

"With my wife."

"She's here for observation."

"What sort of observation?"

"Well," he said, and he picked up his pipe. "Various sorts. But since we do not have a confidentiality statement signed, I 'm afraid that's all I can say."

"What is a confidentiality statement?"

"It is a statement your wife must sign that will allow me to discuss her case with you. You see, everything we say up here is confidential."

"Why won't she sign it?"

"Oh, I didn't say she wouldn't sign it. I haven't asked her yet."

"Doctor, where are you going with this conversation?"

He lit the pipe and expelled aromatic vanilla Cavendish

into the room.

"The thing is, you see, I'd like to run some tests and observe your wife for a few days."

"So?"

"I need your permission."

"My permission? What about Charlene's permission?"

"You are her husband. You have the authority to admit her for observation."

"I do?"

"Yes."

"But I don't have permission to know what's going on with her?"

"That's correct."

"That's crazy," I said.

"We don't use that word up here, Daniel. May I call you Daniel? The fact is, I can keep her here for three days without anyone's permission if I see fit."

"You threatening me?"

"Not at all, Daniel. You see, your wife was brought here for other than physical reasons."

"What reasons?"

"Her conversation with police led them to question her competence. Now if she were violent, against herself or against another, we would automatically hold her. But she is quite peaceful."

"Then you must tell me what her problem is."

"We don't know. Parts of her conversation were

reported as aberrant. That can be a simple matter of momentary stress, or it might suggest something more."

"Like what?"

"Many things. We can give her tests. Talk with her. Observe her behavior. In a few days we might know more."

"I can't make a decision like that," I said. "You'll have to ask Charlene."

He stored his pipe in a wooden bowl.

"I do wish you would reconsider."

"I'm not putting my wife in a place like this if she doesn't want to be here."

"Very well," he said.

He went to the door.

"Will you join us now, Mrs. Reed?"

Charlene came in and sat in the chair next to me.

"You okay?" I asked.

"Yes. But I do not like this place. I want to go home."

"Charlene, this is Doctor Leonard."

"We've met."

She looked at him with severe dislike.

"Mrs. Reed," Doctor Leonard asked, "may I speak freely in front of your husband?"

Charlene nodded.

"I believe you might have experienced a schizoid event. I would like you to stay in our care for a few days so we can run some tests."

"I don't know what you're talking about. I'm a pregnant

woman. I cannot be put through tests. The baby will suffer."

She implored me.

"Please, Daniel. Our baby."

"Okay, Doctor, that's enough. She's obviously upset, but staying here will make her more upset. She's over-stressed, as you suggested. She's pregnant. We've had some financial struggles. I'll take her home. She can rest there. She'll be fine."

"Very well, then," Doctor Leonard said, and he stood. "I'll make the arrangements."

Chapter 27

Denial provides an exquisite elixir, and I accepted its addictive blindness. We didn't want to know about mental illness because we didn't want to believe in it. Therefore, it didn't exist. If it did exist, it belonged to those illnesses that other people get. A dead body in the trunk? I didn't want to think about it. The mafia? Of course, I'm not Mafioso, but Charlene's intuition hit close. Although I didn't work for the mafia, turns out I had partnered with a crook.

The days and nights of the business flowed together like droplets coalescing to a puddle, a muddled disarray of similar and repeated events which occupied my time and my mind. Other concerns became relegated to secondary importance, a necessary adjunct to the pride of owning my own business. I worked so hard and so faithfully that time passed without its daily recognition, and as the first two months of operation passed into the third, I began to establish both a sense of confidence in and a positive expectation for the future. The first quarter of the new year was coming quickly, and I began to look forward to my first fat quarterly bonus.

When I arrived at work early Saturday morning, I was pleased by an unexpected visit from Bob. Our business relationship teetered toward friendship, and I felt that in time we would, in fact, become friends.

"What's the occasion?" I asked.

He sat on a bar stool, and wiped sweat from his forehead.

"Have a beer and take a load off," I said. I drew two cold drafts. "What's up?"

Bob took a long, healthy drink, and put the glass down in front of him. He opened his sales book and pulled two invoices from the pocket. Both invoices were for beer deliveries, one for Whispers and one for The Bistro du Vin.

"Take a look," he said.

"What am I looking for?" I asked.

"You're the business genius," he said and lifted his drink.

I perused the sheets.

"Are these the same brands of beer for The Bistro and for here?"

"Yep."

"The prices per case are different."

"Yep."

"What's going on, Bob?"

"Daniel, I like you. I've seen you work your tail off to make something of this place. I'll probably lose my job for telling you this, but you need to know. You need to get out, move on, cut your losses and get away from this guy."

I refilled his glass. I walked around the bar, locked the door, turned off the OPEN sign. When I sat down, I lifted my glass.

"I appreciate that you're my friend," I said. "I don't

know if I'm going to appreciate what you have to say."

"Yeah."

Bob obviously had not practiced his speech.

"Here's the thing, Ronaldo has a gambling bug. Has for years. A while back he drew an unlucky streak and ended up owing a large sum to people who have various ways of collecting their money. Let's just say their methods fall outside the norm of regular collection agencies. Ronaldo's wife is the brains of their business, and she always paid his debts. But when he started losing big, she cut him off. Rather than breaking his knee caps, the people he owes the money to came up with this business scam."

"Scam?"

"You never see the bills because they go directly to the accountant. Whispers pays, on paper, two times what we charge everyone else. The difference, the money that the accountant puts in the ledger, actually goes to pay off Ronaldo's debt."

"I don't get it, Bob. I mean, the business must pay the amount on the bills or there would be a big accounting problem. Right?"

Bob looked at me as if I were a child. "So?"

"Well, how does the accountant use that extra money to pay Ronaldo's gambling debt if the company pays the bill amount?"

Bob slugged the rest of his beer. "I can't draw you a picture. You figure it out. Keep in mind that these bills and these debts never go through any banks. You run a mostly cash business. Think about it. You'll see the light."

Youth possesses some ability to grasp the wickedness of greed, but it remains generally an unspoken topic, like mental illness. At that point it didn't seem worth it to explain to Bob that I was expecting a big bonus at the end of the quarter.

"Bob, any chance you could lose those invoices? Maybe back by the cooler some place? I need to talk to Ronaldo."

"What invoices?" Bob asked. "You know I don't leave invoices here. They go directly to the accountant."

"Thanks," I said.

He nodded. I unlocked the door, and he left. That was the last time I ever saw him.

I had to act. I closed up the bar, pocketed the invoices, and decided to confront Ronaldo directly. I drove to his home.

Ronaldo and Patricia lived at the end of a cul-de-sac, in an expensive neighborhood, in one of the older developments at the top of the hill at the north end of town. When I arrived, however, I could not get to their driveway for the congregation of parked vehicles, including three police cars and an ambulance. I walked to the house. I met Mr. Pallagrini, Ronaldo's attorney, in the front yard.

"What are you doing here?" he asked without saying hello.

"I want to see Ronaldo. He's been cheating me."

"You found out? How? Well, it doesn't matter. Everything is changed. Ronaldo has been shot."

"Shot?"

"Yes."

"Shot?"

"By a jealous husband. Evidently, he followed his wife here. One of Renaldo's afternoon trysts. Walked right into the unlocked house, into the bedroom, and caught them in the act."

"Killed him?"

"No. Would have been easier for everyone if he had. He was so enraged, he shot three times, twice into the bed and once into Ronaldo's shoulder. He'll live. Odd man. When he saw the blood, he looked at his wife, lowered the gun, walked to the living room, and called 911. Waited on the couch. Still had the gun in his hand when the police arrived. He offered no resistance, but perhaps because of the gun they were excessively physical with him. Unnecessarily so. Probably has grounds for a brutality suit, if he wishes."

"Mr. Pallagrini, Ronaldo has been shot?"

"It's not surprising, really. We have advised him against his behavior often enough. But here we are. Mrs. Giordano has closed your business, and we must discuss your future. Would you like to meet at the accountant's office?"

Too much information in too short a period of time can overwhelm the brain. When this happens, it generally ceases the process of active thought and moves to an activity similar to an automobile on cruise control. As everyone knows, changes in the intensity of cerebral stimuli result in a change in the firing rate of nerve impulses. Scientists refer to this action as neuroadaptation, and my brain was neuro adapting by advising me to sit down, which I did.

"This might be a shock to you, Daniel, but trust me, there's nothing further to be done here. We have extensive paperwork to process. Won't you meet me and Mr. Wilshire at his office in an hour?"

"Okay," I said, still in a fog. "But, Mr. Pallagrini, I want to know everything."

"Of course," he said. "In an hour then. You remember the location?"

I nodded. The shade of the curb trees cooled my skin, and the rustling of the leaves quieted my anger impulses to the point where I began to breathe with less constriction. The ambulance left. The police cars took off with the suspect. The neighbors milled around, talking.

I stopped for a cup of coffee. My brain wanted to think, but I told it to take a nap. I felt like I had landed on the wrong side of a tormented dream. The changes of my worldscape made me dizzy. I drank the coffee black, and it burned my tongue. The attorney, Pallagrini, greeted me when I opened the office door.

"Ah, Mr. Reed, may I get you some coffee?"

"No. I want to know what the hell is going on."

"Yes, of course. Let us go into the conference room."

We sat at the same table we had signed the contracts.

"Mr. Wilshire is gathering some papers. He'll be along."

I attempted to reveal a stern face. It was not difficult, really. I grew more angry with each minute.

"I apologize for my part in this," Mr. Pallagrini said. He exhaled a sad sigh from his nose. "Nobody suffers like I do, Mr. Reed. I am a sensitive man. My mother wanted me to play the piano. It is not my fault that people get themselves in trouble. Someone must get them out. I do that, and in helping, I am demonized."

The accountant, Mr. Wilshire, entered. He sat next to Pallagrini. They both across the table from me.

"Where shall we begin?" Wilshire said.

"Right here," I said, and I placed the two beer invoices on the table. "I found these in my bar today. Either of you want to explain them?"

"No need to play coy, Mr. Reed," Wilshire said. "Obviously, you're aware of Mr. Geordano's scheme to repay some of his debt, using funds from his bar."

"My bar!" I said. "At least half of it. He can't take more money than I take. We're living on very little right now, and the quarterly bonuses are essential to us. So they must be fair. You're going to pay me the differences in these bills"

"I'm afraid not," Wilshire said. "In fact, I may as well explain your circumstances in full. Mr. Pallagrini will clarify any legal nuances."

Mr. Pallagrini nodded.

"Mr. Geordano, Ronaldo, has a gambling addiction. Mrs. Geordano, Patricia, of course, has known about it, and she has been instrumental in managing these indiscretions. In truth, Patricia Geordano owns all of the Geordano assets."

"What's your point?" I asked.

"The incident today brought Patricia to a crossroads. She must act to protect herself and her holdings."

"Meaning?"

"You know, the possibility of frivolous lawsuits. Also, there might be accusations of a child."

"Or two," Pallagrini added.

"So, of course, she cannot be held liable for Ronaldo any longer. She has closed all joint accounts, taken legal possession of all real estate, and has mitigated losses by filing for divorce."

"As of yesterday," Pallagrini clarified. "For obvious reasons, we will date these actions yesterday, prior to today's incident."

"What does all this mean to me?"

"Since Patricia actually owns all the businesses, and she will, in fact, own everything outright within about 30 days—"

"Ronaldo will not oppose any action," Pallagrini interjected.

"Yes. The thing is, Daniel, Patricia has ordered us to close Whispers. Since Ronaldo has signed a power of attorney naming Patricia, or he will later this evening, after surgery, Mrs. Geordano will proclaim all of your dealings null and void. We have notified all your accounts. The locks are being changed as we speak. Negotiations are under way for a new owner to take possession of the premises at some future date."   ·

"She can't do that."

"I'm afraid she can, Daniel," the attorney assured me.

"She already has," the accountant confirmed.

"What about my bonus?"

"There will be no bonus since the business has not actually made a profit," Wilshire said. "In fact, it hasn't been open a full quarter, so there will be no quarterly report. Only a final accounting."

"But Patricia is not without a heart, Daniel," Pallagrini said. "I have a check here for three thousand dollars. It is yours if you sign this agreement to seek no further compensation regarding the matter of Whispers."

"She can do all this?"

They both nodded.

What choice did I have? I didn't have the money to hire an attorney, even if I did have a chance for damages. Obviously, they had already covered all their bases, or they were in the process of getting them taken care of. We absolutely needed the money.

I signed the agreement which dissolved our partnership and which essentially bought my silence for three thousand bucks. I put the check in my wallet and prepared to leave.

"There is one more detail, Mr. Reed," Pallagrini said.

I looked at him.

"Under the circumstances, the bank has called the loan."

"What loan?"

"The one hundred and twenty thousand dollar tenant renovation loan."

"I'm not paying that. Patricia owns everything. She has a new buyer. Let them pay it. It belongs to them."

"Not legally," Pallagrini said. "You are the only signatory to the loan agreement. You must pay."

I sat down. "How am I supposed to do that?" I asked them both.

Pallagrini looked at Wilshire. They nodded to one another. Then Pallagrini looked at me.

"We're not without hearts, either, Daniel," he said. "Alexander and I believe that we can arrange for a bankruptcy. It will clear you of all your debt, including the bank note."

"Bankruptcy?"

"And we will provide you our services for half what we normally charge in a case like this. For you, only thirty-five hundred dollars."

I should have stayed in school.

Chapter 28

Charlene took the news of our bankruptcy poorly. She slid from morose sadness into uncomfortable depression. I don't blame her. Bankruptcy inflicts humiliation and shame, and it shatters one's dignity in the process. I felt as if I had failed all the promises of America. That I had squandered all the potential of the California dream. I failed Charlene, and I failed our baby. I did not realize, or I did not want to realize, that I also failed myself.

I gave my energies to the pursuit of money, a thing, an inanimate object unable to provide affection. Wealth cannot even hold one's hand. Never grew hands, I guess, like those potato road kill that never learned to grow legs.

I tried to address my mad dash for wealth. I asked myself: why do I want to be rich? I knew the answer. I wanted Charlene and our child to be comfortable, financially safe. In constructing the empire of a business, financial safety became a commandment to accumulate wealth. It is as if I accepted Ronaldo's subliminal imperative that being a millionaire equaled being wealthy, and the notion that unremembered hours of hard work would, in fact, transform the ideal into the real. The thing is, wealth accumulation becomes a never-ending process. No matter how much money lands in the vault, no matter how many hours one works, the process must continue. In other words, there's never enough.

Chapter 29

The bank, the businesses, and their attorneys began harassment immediately. We received notices of demand in the mail and phone calls at all hours of the day and night. Collection agents would stop by our house, and Charlene began to lock all the doors and windows. She unplugged the phone. She never turned lights on, nor did she ever again open our drapes. She used small candles to make her way around the house. She began to lose weight.

One afternoon, as I rested on the couch, the doorbell rang. I peered out the corner of the window and saw the Sears delivery truck. I didn't think it was possible, but maybe Charlene had ordered more furniture. I decided to tell them we couldn't afford it. Whatever it was, it had to go back.

I opened the door, and one of the two guys handed me an invoice with a black stamp across the face that read NOTICE.

"Look, you guys," I said, "we can't afford whatever this is. I'm sorry, but you'll have to take it back."

"This is not a delivery," the guy said. "We're here to pick up a dining room set and some bedroom furniture."

"What is it, Daniel?" Charlene asked from behind the wall in the kitchen.

"I'm not sure," I called to her.

"What do you mean?" I asked the men.

"It's on the paper. You're in default for non-payment. Look, we're just the pick-up guys. Can we come in?"

"Hang on," I said. "Give me a minute."

I went to Charlene.

"Honey, this paper says that since we've missed our payments, they're here to repossess the furniture."

"How can that be?" she asked.

"We're filing for bankruptcy. We're not paying any of our bills. Remember what the attorney told us?"

"I'm pretty sure I paid them."

"No, we didn't pay them, and we must let them take the furniture."

"I won't let them take my baby's room. No."

I tried to comfort her, but she turned away from me, sullen and cold.

"Do you know the main road kill in Maine?"

"I don't care what the main road kill in Maine is," I snapped. She stopped. She stood straight. Her eyebrows raised in surprise. Her mouth hung open.

"I'm sorry," I said. "What is the main road kill in Maine?"

"Captain said you would react this way. It's because you don't love me. And whether or not you care, the main road kill in Maine is moose. Or mooses."

The men worked quickly and silently. They carried the kitchen table together, turning it on edge to squeeze through the doorway. We watched them carry the table to the van. They returned, and each one grabbed two chairs and brought them to the street.

Being a good Californian, I did not know our neighbors well. Nevertheless, several of them walked to the front of their yards to watch.

"We need the bedroom things," the guy said.

I led them down the hall to the baby's room. I switched the light, and the joyfulness of the room appeared, filled with the memories of preparation and the excitement of expectation.

The men began to disassemble the little bed.

Suddenly, Charlene ran into the room and pulled one of the men by his arm.

"No," she screamed.

I hugged her, thin and fragile, but she pulled away with the fury of a mother to be.

"How can you let them take my baby's bed?"

She went down the hall. We all heard the bedroom door slam.

"Our first child," I explained. "A girl."

"We're just the pick up guys, man. Nothing we can do."

I nodded.

They unscrewed the angel-mobile from the headboard and handed it to me. I held the mobile as if it were our baby. I felt thunder in my chest, a loud catastrophe of deep, invisible clamor. I could not breathe. I could not speak. I could not, dared not, look into tomorrow.

As the two men dismantled the bed, they made the process look mechanical, but to me it felt more like destruction than repossession. We had imagined Ella in that bed so often that as they carried it out of the room, it seemed like they were taking Ella too.

I removed the few clothes, the bathing towels, and the little toys from the dresser. I put them on the floor in a pile. They sat quietly in the corner like a scolded child.

Finally, they took the rocker. I looked at the empty space and I wondered: where will I sit to hold my snuggling child?

The room changed. Emptied of its promise, it held only bankrupt expectations, like ghosts.

Oh, God. Charlene.

I went to our bedroom and tapped at the door.

Charlene sat on the side of the bed, her hands folded, resting on her lap. She had pulled the drapes aside, and she looked out the window. With sad eyes, she watched the white van pull away from the curb. It looked as if a part of her left with the truck, and it pained her.

I put my arms around her. She let me hold her.

Chapter 30

The next day, the furniture company came to reclaim the couch. We kept the bed because I used some of the three thousand dollars to pay it off. Charlene continued to sleep there alone. I slept on our old chair, or when my back hurt, on the floor.

That afternoon I met with Mr. Pallagrini and Mr. Wilshire. They accepted as a down payment, five hundred dollars which I also took from the three thousand dollar buyout. They provided a list of records they needed in order to gather our financial life to hand over to a bankruptcy judge.

I drove home slowly. We still had the car, at least for awhile. I thought about stopping at the secondhand store, but I had no energy for shopping. It's exhausting to search an unknowable future. When I entered the house, Charlene met me at the door.

"I'm going to spend the night at Odette's."

"That's a good idea," I said. "A little change. A little company."

She did not want to talk.

"Would you mind," I asked, "if I invite Mark over for a game of chess?"

"I don't really care," she said, and she walked out the door to wait for Odette.

Her future remained as unknowable as mine, and she

would not talk to me. Maybe a night off with Odette would help. Maybe a night of chess with Mark would do me some good, too.

I called him.

He said, "Great."

Mark entered a house of sparse furnishings that evening.

He produced an unopened bottle of twenty-five year old Scotch whiskey.

I retrieved ice in a bowl, two glasses, and paper towels. Picking up ice cubes can cause undesirable moisture on the fingertips during a chess match.

I brought out my Mexican black and white onyx, hand carved chess set, a holdover totem from my single days. We used a TV tray for a table. I sat on a wooden stool, ceding the living room chair to Mark. As I set the board, Mark mixed a small portion of ice with a generous portion of Scotch in each glass.

"Been a while," he said.

He handed me one of the glasses and sat back, performing his leisurely cigarette lighting ceremony. He exhaled gray smoke and raised his hand in a gesture of salute. I matched the gesture, and we drank. I enjoyed the liquid contentment that slid into my belly.

"Danny boy, I have news."

"Oh?"

"Vivien and I have decided to tie the knot."

"It has been a while."

He jiggled his drink to make the ice tingle, and the music of alcoholic melancholia played gently against the silence of the house. He observed the glass a moment, or its contents, and as suddenly as the first snow appears in late fall, he downed the contents and poured himself another, adding one single piece of ice.

"Good stuff," I said. "My compliments to the chef."

"I don't know if I told you that Vivian has a seven year old daughter."

"I don't think you've mentioned that before. And frankly, I'm glad we are having this discussion while Charlene is visiting Odette. That sisterhood of theirs puts a lot of pressure on me to steer you onto a path back to Odette."

"No doubt."

"In fact, I don't know how Charlene will react to the news of your marriage. I wouldn't count on her attendance."

He nodded in the affirmative and lifted the bottle.

"Let me top that off," he said, and he refilled my half empty glass. "I wouldn't want to cause you any more burden than you already carry."

"Hey, what are friends for? Charlene won't like it, but she'll understand."

"Are you sure, Daniel? She's been re-inventing strange behavior these few months. I don't know."

"She'll be fine. As long as you and Vivian are okay that she won't attend the services, your best man will be there."

The subtle drunkenness of good Scotch began to ensue, that soft tingling of the skin, that comfortable relaxation of tension. We sat silently, pondering our drinks. Pool is my game, but I felt so comfortable, I figured I might win a chess match this night.

Mark revived each glass again, and I reached for a black and white pawn.

"Pick a hand," I said.

"Hold on a bit longer," Mark said. "About that best man thing."

"Yes?"

"Ain't gonna happen. I feel bad, but Vivian wants her brother to be the best man. Nothing I can do."

"You serious?"

"Afraid so."

"I understand. Family and all. It's okay. But it's going to feel strange sitting in the audience instead of standing at your side."

Mark took a long drag on his cigarette.

"That's the other news, Amigo," he said, exhaling the words within the midst of sinuous smoke.

"Oh?"

"You aren't invited to the wedding."

"Not invited?"

"No. You see, Vivian thinks you're a bad influence on

me."

"How so?"

"It's not your fault, really. But we are best friends, and you do, or you did, own a bar."

"How are those things bad?"

"They're not bad. Not bad at all. It's just that I may have used them as excuses on an occasion or two."

"What do you mean?"

"I might have told Vivian I needed to take care of you from time to time. You know, nights I came around late, or not at all. I told her you have a drinking problem, and since we're best friends, I needed to be there for you."

"How nice."

"Anyhow, she's decided we shouldn't pal around anymore, and she insists that you stay away from the wedding."

"Insists?"

"Afraid so."

I stared at the chess board. What could I do?

"No hard feelings, buddy?" Mark said. He lifted his glass across the table.

"No hard feelings."

"Women. What are you going to do?"

"Yeah," I said.

But I knew what I was going to do. I planned to beat him three games in a row, and I planned to make sure he left that night with an empty bottle of twenty-five year old

Scotch.

And I did.

Chapter 31

Mark's marriage happened pretty fast; so fast I didn't see it. That's a little sarcasm. I realize I shouldn't hold a grudge, but, really, how does a man not invite his best friend to his wedding? Isn't marriage supposed to create bonds, not destroy them?

Doctor Leonard felt that my anger was misdirected, that I was really angry at the impending bankruptcy. That in fact, I was really angry at Ronaldo, but I'm too kind a person, and I couldn't hold that particular anger because he had been shot and I felt sorry for him. He was wrong, of course. None of my angers were misdirected, not my anger at Mark, nor at Ronaldo, nor at the bankruptcy. I was angry at them all.

The buttress of a man's will is anchored in his convictions, and convictions proceed from experience. For instance, when I was eight years old, my mother caught me crying outside my hideout back near the bushes that grew along our back yard.

"What's the matter, baby?" she asked me.

"I'm not a baby. Leave me alone."

To my surprise, she did. She got up from the grass and walked into the house. So I followed her.

She poured a glass of cold milk and sat at the table. I sat in the chair next to her and gulped the milk.

"My," she said, "that's a man-sized swallow."

"Teresa Jardine called me ugly," I said.

"Oh."

"I told her she stinks."

"That should settle things," she comforted.

I looked at her.

"Why?" I asked.

"You got even. Isn't that what you wanted?"

 "Not really," I admitted.

"What did you want?"

I wanted her to like me, but I did not know that at the time. I knew I was angry at her. That's what I knew.

My mother tried to help me resolve my confusion toward Teresa Jardine by suggesting that I talk to her, to tell her she hurt my feelings.

I walked to her yard and called out. "Hey, Teresa." She came out onto the porch.

"You hurt my feelings," I said.

"Good."

"It doesn't matter," I informed her. "You're just a girl."

Although we lived in the same neighborhood all the years of our childhood, Teresa and I never became friends.

"Well, what did you learn?" my mother asked when I returned home.

"I learned to keep quiet," I said and went to my room.

I stayed in my room the rest of the day, but at darkness, I crawled out the window. Our back yard met up with a small hill, and I walked into the cavernous fortress of the trees.

The codification of humiliation and uncertainty in human relationships does not generally clarify itself during childhood. Instead, the brain waits patiently for adult lessons before the philosophical importance of these concepts become repeated, and thus, relevant. Childhood exists as a time of fallowness, like the earth, a time when seeds planted take root beneath the surface, waiting in the substrate of the fecund brain-mulch we call the unconscious for the right moment to sprout wisdom. That night, wrapped within the confines of rustling trees, moon white darkness, and a childhood wound, I languished in the sweet rebellion of escape and solitude. During the course of that long night, I learned to fear humiliation and to despise myself whenever it landed on me, like one learns during potty-training that if he does not get the excrement in the toilet, he must despise himself when it lands instead on him.

The other wonderful power of childhood grants the brain permission to forget.

By the next morning, I felt fine, although I walked far aside whenever Teresa Jardine came into view. I forgot those lessons from one small childhood day and one secret childhood night, but the seeds merely went fallow. It seemed to me, upon recollection, that all those lessons, unconscious and emotional, finally blossomed with the passing of my friend's unseen wedding and as the recognition of our impending court date took root.

Charlene grew more distraught, and we met with her OBGYN. He spoke to us in his office.

"Charlene, you are very depressed. You are not eating. And you tell me that you are not sleeping well. I could prescribe drugs; however, they can cause dangerous complications during pregnancy, and I advise against them."

"What can we do?" I asked.

"She needs rest. Complete rest. I know of an excellent facility. It's a little costly, but the staff are first class. Good food, no stressors, plenty of rest. All under a doctor's supervision."

"How long a rest?" I asked.

"I think two weeks will make all the difference. At the most, three."

"What do you mean by costly?"

"A thousand dollars a week. I know that might be substantial, but I feel Charlene needs it. She must rest and regain her strength."

"I understand," I said. "Thank you."

"Yes. Let me know, and I'll take care of the paperwork."

In the car, I lowered my head to the steering wheel.

"Of course, we can't afford it," Charlene said. She lit a cigarette.

"Smoking's probably not good for the baby," I said.

"Don't tell me what to do. That's your problem, always

spying on me, telling me what to do."

"Charlene, please," I put my hand on her lap, but she pushed it away.

Later that evening, I made a decision to ask for help.

I hadn't spoken to my father in a number of years. After my mother died, he abandoned me. Not physically, but emotionally. He worked long hours. He did pay for house-sitters, but none of them stayed long, so I did not make friends with any. He reconciled his grief by immersing his energy in work. Maybe I inherited that habit from him. When I left for California the summer I graduated from high school, he hardly noticed, just as he didn't notice I needed him when my mother left me.

I phoned him.

"Dad, it's Daniel."

"Daniel. Nice surprise."

"Yeah."

"How you doing?"

"Good. Well, pretty good, but I've got a problem. That's why I called."

"What is it?"

I explained Charlene's condition and her need for rest.

"I'd like to borrow the two thousand dollars. I'll pay you back, I promise."

"That sounds bad, Daniel, and I'd like to help, but, well, you know, I'm re-married."

"We're talking about your grandchild here," I said.

"Samantha has three children still living at home. Oh yeah, I married a young one. But, you're married too, so you know. We each take care of our own."

I didn't say anything.

"She's your wife, right? Okay. It was good talking to you. Stay in touch now, you hear?"

Chapter 32

We did not send Charlene to a rest home, but I did attempt to keep the struggles of the bankruptcy process from her. I bought a used couch, a small kitchen table with two chairs. I found a stroller and a basinet at a yard sale that were in good condition. I stored them in Ella's room. These gestures did not make a meaningful impression on Charlene.

About a week before the court date, I received a call from Odette.

"Daniel, come home right now."

"What's wrong?"

"It's Charlene. Hurry."

I had gotten a job waiting tables and washing dishes at a neighborhood diner. My new boss did not like the fact that I took time off, but the procedures for the bankruptcy were insistent, and Charlene's needs demanded immediacy. When I told him I needed to go home in the middle of my shift, he fired me.

Gray and black bulbous clouds swirled like a menacing caldron of witches' mischief and blurred the afternoon sky. Lightning flashed, startling and ominous, like a white, electric wave along the near horizon. The after-light of the flash faded, and thunder, like a sudden explosion, rumbled into the distance. Suddenly, like loosening a tourniquet from the clouds, rain fell in plunging droplets, seething

with energy. I let the pellets blow in through the open
window, and they wet my hair and stung my face, cooling
momentarily the frantic thoughts in my head.

I rushed through the rain into the house.

Odette sat at the kitchen table.

"I brought carrots," Odette said, pointing to a bag on
the table. "I found her like this. She won't talk to me."

Charlene's face looked dull, like oxidized pewter. Her
dark hair was dry and stuck out like straw, brittle and
mean. She looked straight ahead, eyelids unblinking as if
terrified. She walked back and forth in front of the sink
with tiny, shuffling steps. She held a brown twig in one
hand. It looked like the spine of a sun-baked bonsai tree,
straight-trunked and without leaves. The dead bark had
tiny ashen streaks. She squeezed it inside her fist, like one
holds a candle.

"Daniel, what's wrong with her?"

"I don't know."

I went to Charlene, and she stopped walking.

"Honey, Odette is here. Look, she brought carrots."

The green walls and the green tiles and the odd
behavior of my wife dominated my mind, like a green
exasperation of vertigo. Charlene's eyes retained that
distant look. Without prelude, she began to speak while
white bubbles of saliva oozed from the side of her mouth.
Her voice sounded disconnected and mesmeric, like cold
mercury.

"I had a cousin named Sylvester, and he went away."

She clung to her twig.

"Where did he go?" Odette asked.

"He had a truck. It had a loud muffler. Every night he would start his truck and listen to the noise. He made it sound like the truck was going very fast. Vroom. Vroom."

She pulled the twig close to her breast and covered one hand with the other.

"Do you miss him?" I asked.

"His days were empty, but every night he started his truck so he could make noise. That was the only power he had. The neighbors complained because he made his noise when they were trying to sleep. Aunt and Uncle sent the truck away. Sylvester cried. He cried and he cried and he stopped eating. Then Aunt and Uncle sent him away."

She brought the twig to her ear as if listening for its voice.

"You're going to send me away, too, aren't you?"

"No, Charlene. Is that what you're worried about? You're not going away, and neither am I. Don't worry about that. I'll never leave you. I promise."

She stopped talking, but a promise only grows truthful with time, so she could make no comment on my ability to keep it. She held her twig and looked off into an unseen vista where she remained motionless and with no further speech.

"Daniel, do something," Odette said.

"What?" I asked, exasperated. "What can I do?"

"I don't know. Maybe take her to the hospital."

"What will they do?"

"I don't know," Odette raised her voice. "Look at her. We've got to do something."

She got off the chair and went to Charlene. She hugged her.

"It's okay, Honey. It's okay. We're going to help you. It's okay."

Odette looked at me.

"Well?" she said.

"Okay. Let's take her to the hospital."

I drove to the emergency room, and Odette held Charlene's hand. The intake took some time, and they didn't want to do too much because we had no insurance. By chance, the nurse who led me to see Doctor Leonard happened to be on duty that night. As she walked down the hallway, she recognized us, and she called Doctor Leonard.

When he arrived, we told him about Charlene's behavior, and he made arrangements to admit Charlene to the sixth floor.

"She needs complete rest," he told us. "You may visit her tomorrow."

"No drugs," I said to him.

"Mr. Reed, I'm the doctor."

"She's pregnant."

"Anyone can see that. She's also in extreme stress. She

must have a sedative."

"A mild one."

He frowned at me.

"Please help her," I said.

Chapter 33

I saw again the terror on her face as strangers led her away to lock her within a world away from me, without me, lost to me. I imagined her shuffling in uncoordinated steps down that dreary hallway beyond locked doors. I feared she would regain normalcy, looking around to find a foreign landscape, but she would not find me, and she would be afraid, and her fear would be my fault because I was not there to protect her.

I went home to an empty house with its silence, its shadows, and its memories. I turned off all the lights and lay on the couch, my arm across my eyes, my mind swirling in the incomprehensible vortex of unprepared-for loss. I understood none of the complexities at work within the psychological patterns and the neurological chemistry of Charlene's mind and body. My solitude stemmed from the fact that I expected her to return to the pattern of completeness we provided one another. I wanted to hold her so that we would occupy our space, safe and in love, in spite of all the foul misery the world can churn. I wanted our life back.

The next day, I returned to the hospital, but when I went to see Charlene, she would not allow my visit.

"Why not?" I asked Doctor Leonard.

"She's very tired, Daniel. She needs rest."

"Why won't she see me?"

"I cannot say as yet. She may have a variety of reasons, but she cannot express them at this time. We must honor her request. Go home now, and get some rest yourself. Over time, you will learn that the consequences of Charlene's pathology are shared."

"What does that mean?"

"It means you need rest, too."

I did not want to leave. I did not want Charlene to dismiss me. I did not want to hear about pathologies or any other path. I wanted a direct path back to our life.

At home, I did not rest. I paced the house. I looked in on our baby's room. I had added a used bed, and I was keeping an eye out for a used rocking chair. I went to our bedroom and stared at our bed. I thought about our first night on the floor, and buying the mattress. I remembered the nights of love-making, of growing comfortable with her presence next to me, warm, solid, confirming my own existence. I could not develop any thought which did not in some way include her, and every memory magnified my aloneness. Our union, however imperfect, re-made me. I did not recognize myself as a singular entity, could not resign my will to unfettered days.

Even tears did not satisfy me.

Finally, night covered the house. I lay on the couch. I slumbered, but I could not sleep. I missed her, and the night dragged on. Sometime after midnight, I left the couch and drove to the hospital. I parked in the parking lot across the roadway. I sat on the hood of the car to search the windows along the line of the sixth floor. I pulled my knees into my chest and stared, hoping that she might disturb a curtain or lean against a window sill so that I might catch a glimpse of her. I watched for her shadow, for any expression of her form.

At some point, two police cars drove up behind my car. Two officers with weapons drawn moved, one to each side of me, and demanded that I stand. I looked from one to the other and eased off the car with my hands up.

"What are you doing here?" one demanded.

I looked away from him to Charlene's window.

"My wife," I managed. "I'm visiting my wife."

I looked away from them to the hospital and back toward them. And I began to cry.

The two policemen backed off a little until I stopped crying.

The older officer holstered his pistol. He nodded to the younger one. He returned to his patrol car and left.

I leaned against the hood of the car, and again gazed up to the sixth floor.

"What's wrong with your wife?" the officer asked.

Everyone knows that California cops believe in their own superiority, and their arrogance is legendary. But this guy listened patiently as I explained Charlene. I felt consoled that another human being, in listening to me, might bear some of my grief.

"You know," he said when I finished, "you can't do anything for her right now. And you're breaking the law loitering here at this time of night."

I nodded.

"Go home now, and get some sleep. You need to take care of yourself if you plan to take care of your wife."

I realized he was right. Unexpectedly, he put his hand on my shoulder.

"Are you okay to drive?"

"Yes," I said. "I'm okay."

"All right, then. Go home. And drive safely."

"Yes, sir," I said. "Thank you for not shooting me."

It was a strange experience being encouraged by a cop. I didn't realize the powerful need I carried for human company. And I began also to understand the will we all carry to give comfort, even to strangers.

Chapter 34

I thought the long morass of loneliness ended when Charlene returned home. Her presence transformed the space of an otherwise empty house to the renewed cadences of sound in the air, comfort in a chair, the smell of vitality within the steam of morning coffee.

Mr. Pallagrini insisted that both Charlene and I attend court, and I tried to prepare Charlene for the schedule of events.

"He promised it would not take long," I told her. "The paperwork has already been submitted and reviewed. The hearing is a formality."

"They will torture you," she said.

"No, they won't. They don't do that anymore. And they won't put us in a poor house. Businesses will not grant us credit, and it may be some years before we can buy a house. That's all. We'll be okay."

We had to appear in the old court house in Sacramento. The first thing I noticed was its size; then the great columns; and finally the striking bas-relief of Lady Justice.

Walking up those many steps, moving from perspective to immediacy, the columns felt titanic, competing with the ominous power of mountains. The white brilliance of the sunlit paint added a somber elegance. The height of the doors, like two vertical drawbridges, let us know we were entering a realm of power. Inside the rotunda, with its marble floors, its staggering oak staircase, and its enormous chandelier, like a star captured and brought to captivity, I felt small.

Pallagrini and Wilshire met us in the lobby.

"The judge has been delayed a few minutes. We can wait in this office," Pallagrini told us. He led us to a small waiting room with a table and leather chairs.

"Make yourselves comfortable."

The attorney and the accountant left, and the sepulcher-like denseness of the room reminded us that we did not belong among the great and powerful.

I took Charlene's hand and patted it. I don't know if I attempted to comfort her or to comfort myself. Both, perhaps.

She looked at me and whispered, "A sudden flood came upon the small village, and the woman was ready to give birth."

"What?"

"Captain told me. While I was in the room. In the hospital. I closed my eyes. He made the time go."

I sat more erect, covered her hand with both of mine.

"The people had to climb trees, and the old women took her to the strong branch above the water. They tied her to the branch, and during the night, when the rattle of thunder came, she delivered her baby. She was weak, and they left her legs tied so she would not fall while she fed her infant. When the rain stopped, the lions returned. They smelled the child and surrounded the tree, and the men could not chase them away for their appetites. They growled and paced through the mud and finally a great lioness leapt to the branch and pulled the baby with her guilty mouth. The baby made no sound."

As she finished, Pallagrini opened the door and stretched his head toward us.

"The judge is ready."

We went to a small court room. The judge sat on a dais behind a shiny desk. On one side stood a uniformed police officer with a pistol in his holster. On the other, a young woman pointed to the paperwork on the judge's desk.

We walked behind Pallagrini and Wilshire to a table with four chairs. Several people sat in the audience area, including Mark. Three men sat at a second table near the judge; these were the attorneys and an administrator from the bank.

The officer swore us to tell the truth, so help us God, a strange phrase to add as appendage to an oath. Does it mean help us to tell the truth, God, because we can't do it on our own? Does it mean we will tell the truth even if God Himself enters the room and interrupts proceedings? Or does it mean that we will tell the truth because God is the true judge of human behavior, and this human assemblage of grandiose architecture and law and social discipline merely attempts to suggest the timber of authority we will meet in heaven? The possibilities invited more thought, but

the judge interrupted my curiosity and ordered Charlene
and me to sit in two chairs that were placed on a raised
platform situated next to the judge's bench.

I rose, but Charlene would not.

"Come on, Honey. We have to move."

She refused.

"Mrs. Reed," the judge said, "will you please take the
stand with your husband?"

Charlene looked at the judge, a vague fear in her eyes.
The difficulty of the long days of this legal process and the
tension in the court evidently bothered her more than I
anticipated.

"Come on, Honey," I said. "Let's go sit up there."

She took my hand. She looked cumbersome as we
walked toward the chairs, with her pregnancy and her
fragile state of mind. When we arrived at the step in front
of the witness box, Charlene sat down on the step. She
would go no further. She grabbed the lapel of her jacket and
held it with both hands.

I looked to the judge, and she gestured for me to sit in
one of the chairs. She took a long look at Charlene, and
during that pause, the courtroom grew quiet.

"Will you answer on behalf of your wife?" she asked me.

"Yes, ma'am."

"Gentlemen," she addressed the attorneys, "you will
refrain from questioning Mrs. Reed. All questions will be
directed to Mr. Reed only."

The ceremony of law pleases only lawyers. It is incessant, tedious play in contrast to the intricate and complex preparations that lead up to it. As the attorney read the list of our debts, the dates of their inception, and the names of businesses and individuals and corporations so indebted, even I fell into a bored repetitiveness.

"Did you, sir, incur the debt of two hundred and seventy-six dollars for a brown and green sofa from Sofa City?"

"Yes, sir."

"Did you incur said debt on the date of December 9th?"

"Yes, sir."

On and on.

When we finished itemizing and confirming all debts, the attorney listed our assets, some of which we were allowed to keep, such as our dishes and our paid-for furniture.

Charlene sat without sound or movement throughout the ordeal, as if she had turned comatose.

When the attorney reached the matter of the car, Mark raised his hand.

"Yes?"

Mark wore a suit, a white shirt, and a tie. He looked like one of the lawyers.

"Mark Sandowski, your Honor."

"Yes, Mr. Sandowski."

"We request that Mr. Reed be allowed to make up his

missed payments, and that way he can keep his car. Everybody needs a good car, your Honor."

"A noble notion, Mr. Sandowski, but that is an option you must discuss in private, not in my court room, and not until the final order of bankruptcy is filed."

"Yes, your Honor."

He sat.

The attorneys for the bank asked for a copy of the final discharge.

"So noted," the judge said.

"Mr. Pallagrini?"

"So noted, your Honor."

Finally, it ended.

The judge thanked me. The attorneys gathered their papers. Pallagrini and Wilshire said they would be in touch.

Mark waited for us.

"My boss thought it would be a good idea for me to get this experience. You know, watching a bankruptcy."

"Yeah," I said. I held Charlene's hand, and we began to move past him, but he stopped us.

"That idea of catching up payments was mine," he said. "Boss said to talk to you about it. I figure you need the car."

"Not right now, Mark. Charlene is tired. We need to get home. I appreciate the offer. We'll talk about it."

Chapter 35

The next day, I met Mark for lunch at The Diner. He waited for me at the back booth.

"Coffee," he said, pointing to a cup across from him. He sipped his own. "Tough go yesterday."

"Yeah."

We ordered sandwiches. I smoked a cigarette while we waited. I didn't know how to place Mark anymore. We lived different lives in different worlds, it seemed. I had not expressed my discomfort with him about his women, though he was now married. I figured it was his business. Besides, he did seem to be settling down. Vivian appeared to provide stability.

"How's business?" I asked.

"I checked this out with our attorney. Since you filed for bankruptcy, and you listed us, we're out the sale and the money. Have to take the car."

"I'm sorry if you lost money, Mark."

"No, listen. After the thing is final, you can make one payment to us, and the contract is valid again. You keep the car. You need a car. And we get paid."

"I appreciate it. But right now things are a mess."

"Tell me about it. Things have gotten strange for me, too."

"How so?"

"Where do I start?"

The waitress brought sandwiches and refilled our cups.

"Sales have been good. I stashed a few bucks, and with Vivian's income, we looked tight."

I nodded and chewed the chicken salad.

"I told you she had a daughter. Great kid. Gonna be somebody one day. Viv thinks so too. That's why she wanted to move up to the northwest school district. Kids need a good education these days, Daniel, and they have the best schools. Houses are pricy, but with both our salaries, we qualified easy for a loan."

"You bought a house?"

"Not the best avenue in town, but only one block over. Closed a week ago," he said. He drank some coffee. "Viv being a single mom, she didn't have any cash for the down payment, so we had to empty my savings to make everything happen. And can you believe this? She wanted new furniture."

"I'm shocked."

He took a bite of his sandwich, and then, still chewing, tore off another bite, a gesture I never saw from him before. In a rush, and still chewing, he said, "But today I got news."

I wiped mayonnaise from the side of my lip.

"What news?" I asked.

"Vivian tendered her resignation today, effective in thirty days."

"Why?"

"I told her we need both our incomes. She surprised me,

twice. First, she has arranged for me to sell cars at the Pontiac dealership."

I saluted this news with my coffee cup. I discovered it empty.

"A friend of her dad owns it. She says I'll make plenty."

"Sounds good," I said, and I motioned for the waitress that we'd like refills.

He looked into his empty cup. As he looked up, the waitress arrived with the pot. Mark did not flirt with her.

As he began adding sugar, I asked, "What's the second surprise?"

He looked at me and dropped the spoon into his brew.

"She said she can't work anymore because she needs time to guide her daughter in school and to take care of the house."

"That is a lot of work," I conceded.

"She said I'll need to make enough for all of us and to pay the child support for Odette's baby."

I put my coffee cup in the saucer.

"How do you think she found out about Odette?" he asked.

He looked like a man who'd been visited by a ghost.

Chapter 36

Charlene, in the final six weeks of her pregnancy, had a few good days. One afternoon she wanted to talk. It was a pleasant change.

She encouraged me in reasoned language to find a better job. I had landed a dish washing job at a working stiff's buffet, but I didn't make much money, minimum wage and no tips.

"It's better than no money," I told her.

"I know, Daniel. But you can do better."

"I'm doing the best I can, Char."

"Daniel."

She paused. She had that look, like I needed instruction.

"Daniel, you have almost three years of college. And you have business experience. More than most."

"Yeah," I said. "I have nearly three months of running my own business, and I know how to go bankrupt."

She did not like that.

"If all you do is feel sorry for yourself, how will you take care of my baby?"

"You mean our baby."

"Well, then?"

"What do you want?"

"Daniel, the baby will be here in a few weeks. We need more money."

"I know. Don't I know?"

"Maybe you can get a job managing a motel or something. It doesn't have to be perfect. Later, maybe you can finish school."

"Would that make you happy?"

"It would make our baby happy."

"Okay. But we have to start talking again," I said.

At that she smiled, and I felt healed. Once rooted, love needs little to re-blossom. We began a new schedule, around my work hours, and we began to try to rebuild our lives.

I applied to several motels, even drove out the back roads to try, but each one phoned quickly to say no. Several weeks into the job search, I drove past a metal building with a painted sign: *Ronni's Pallets*. Uncertain what sort of work occurred within, I acted on a random inclination and went inside.

"I wonder if I could apply for a job?"

"We are not hiring at this time," the secretary said. "We have enough men on the line."

"I'm not looking for line work," I said. "I have management experience, and I have taken some accounting classes at Marysville."

She hesitated.

"Will you ask?"

"Like I said, I don't think we are hiring."

"Could you ask anyway?"

She removed her glasses.

"Please?"

She looked as if she couldn't quite judge me.

"I'll ask," she said.

I sat in the chair. What am I doing, I thought. This is crazy.

After a couple of minutes, an older man, slightly gray, slender and wearing a tie, walked into the waiting area.

"I'm Mr. Ronni," he said. He shook my hand, and his grip said he wasn't just the owner. He obviously worked the line as he built his business.

He invited me to his office.

"Have a seat."

I felt uncomfortable, given that my only experience negotiating a position like this was with Ronaldo, and that didn't work out exactly as planned.

"We're growing," Mr. Ronni said. "I need someone to take care of the books. I have an accountant, but I need someone to keep up day to day activity. Time sheets, income, outgo. You know, make sure the bills get paid on time. That sort of work."

We discussed my experience with the bar and my college classes.

He seemed to like me. He offered me a job as a bookkeeper.

When I got home, I jumped the steps and ran into the house.

"Charlene. I have news."

She sat on the couch, and watched me run past her.

"I'm here, Daniel."

"I got a job."

I told her about Mr. Ronni, making pallets, the office. All of it with one breath.

"I start on Monday. And, I start at ten dollars an hour. I'll be on probation for ninety days. If Mr. Ronni and I both feel the job is working out, he will raise my rate to fifteen dollars an hour. We're going to be okay, Charlene. Everything will be okay."

"Yes," she said, and sipped her tea, more interested in the impending birth than in news of my job. In fact, her body language suggested that she knew weeks ago that the job would show up.

I went to bed in a joyful mood. Isn't it true that on occasion a small victory can portend a momentous tomorrow? I would sleep soundly for the first time in many nights. Around midnight, I rolled over and reached to put my arm around Charlene, but she was gone. Probably in the toilet, I thought. I fluffed the pillow and rolled on to my back to wait for her. I watched the minutes on our illuminated clock tick away, red, digital time, minutes escaping like wishes. Eleven. Twelve. Thirteen.

I began to grow uncomfortable with her absence. Still, she did not return. I decided to check.

The bathroom door was open. Not in there.

I checked the kitchen. Nope.

I found her in the living room, on the floor, her back against the couch.

"What is it?"

"The baby."

I didn't think. I reacted.

"Can you stand if I help you?"

"Daniel, something's happening."

She looked in pain, one hand on her stomach. I reached down for her, and she held my arm.

"Okay," I said. Let's get up."

Together, we stood. We walked gingerly to the car. When she eased into the seat, I noticed blood on her night gown.

"Hold on, Honey. Hold on."

I raced to the emergency room. Once there, nurses helped Charlene into a wheel chair. They rushed her down a long, brightly lit hallway, through a set of double swinging doors, without me.

I went to a waiting area with soft chairs, some magazines on a table, and a TV hanging on the wall. Thankfully, the room was empty. I wanted to be alone. I turned off the TV. I tried to read a magazine, but I could not concentrate. An hour later, the emergency room doctor came to the room.

"Mr. Reed?"

I jumped up. "Yes. I'm Daniel Reed. How is she?"

"Mr. Reed." He paused.

I didn't like the pause. It felt awkward.

"Doctor?" I asked.

"I'm sorry to have to tell you this, Mr. Reed. Your wife delivered a stillborn fetus. There was nothing we could do."

The disbelief on my face must have been obvious.

"Would you like to sit?" he offered.

I sat down.

"Stillborn?"

"Stillborn."

"Dead?"

"I'm sorry. We gave your wife a sedative. You may go to her now, if you wish."

"Doctor?"

"A girl," he said.

I trudged to Charlene's room. The woman in the other bed snored behind the curtain. I sat in the chair at Charlene's bedside.

"Captain found my baby," she said.

"What are you talking about?"

"I tried to tell you, but you would not listen."

I figured she was delusional from the drugs, and in spite of the sedative, she did not sleep. Neither did she again acknowledge my presence. She clutched the sheet in both hands, and she pulled it up around her chin like a cloth shield. She lay the entire night in that position.

Although uninvited, I kept watch with her.

In the morning, made speechless by our grief, we drove

home covered in the shroud of emptiness that descends with the death of a child. Somehow, Ella's loss represented the unlived potential of all that is good. For me, the loss felt like a reprimand at the years I spent in the pitiless exhaustion of unfulfilled ambitions. Worst of all, her death dismantled the future, for both Charlene and I had made and re-made dozens of scenarios regarding our daughter. Yet, before we even got to hold her, she was gone. Though she had never lived within our home, never slept in her used crib, never once kept us up at night crying, we missed her presence, and the lack of it pressed against every wall and every conversation.

I went to work, but the noise of commerce seemed metallic and mundane. The joyful bounce in my step from a few days prior, abandoned me. My feet dragged. I scuffed the tips of my shoes. And my back hurt.

Each evening, my spirit strengthened upon seeing Charlene, and although she remained morose and withdrawn, I made efforts to console her. I brought chocolate. I brought roses. I made tea. It might be true that I performed these gestures as much for myself as for her. I can't say. I know that I desired comforting, yet something, some other force, compelled me to recognize a greater need in Charlene. Somehow, her loss seemed greater, since she carried the infant for many months as a living piece to her own flesh. I considered it perhaps a mother's blessing turned to curse, longing now for an impossible fulfillment.

Such damage changes the brain, changes the heart. No man can comprehend the intimacy of carrying a child from microscopic conception to separate and individuated human life. I know Charlene spoke with the baby while she was in her womb. I know she sang to her.

Such music no longer filled the great void of our home.

I felt the loss too, the loss of the baby and the loss of intimacy that Charlene withheld, a combined loss so great it registered in my body like hunger remembering food, a physical memory transported by the blood to each starving membrane of my stomach and to each solitary synapse of my nerves.

I felt a similar hunger when I was young and I thought of my dead mother. When she left me, when I felt that loss, I cried for her to return. I cried for many days. Then one day, I stopped crying. Something allowed me to continue to live, some genetic desire greater than the loss. I knew, for instance, that I would not meet my dead mother at breakfast or at the park. No. From that point forward, I met the dead only in memory, and the longing was minimized by the hope that one day, under heavenly circumstances, our spirits would unite again.

Eventually, I managed to place Ella in that sacred, secret place with my mother.

I could not touch Ella or my mother, and I could not touch Charlene. She did not permit touch. The loss of someone still alive, however, cannot be relegated to the murky places of memory. The living inhabit each day. You cannot lay to rest that which still breathes. Throughout many days, I clung to the hope of renewing our acquaintance, our friendship. And I missed her in my flesh with the same ferocity I missed my mother and my daughter in my soul.

Chapter 37

Mark called to have lunch.

"How's the new job?" I asked.

"Bigger commissions, bigger dollars."

"I read something about Pontiac having money problems. Production? Unions? Can't remember."

"It's all hype. Makes the stock go down. Those in the know, buy. Those who don't know, sell. It's all about the money."

"And Vivian?"

"Her family's connected. Her father knows a guy who's tight with a stock broker. I'll be getting in soon."

"Sounds good."

"How about you? What's new?"

"Nothing new."

"I can get you on if you want to make some real money."

"Appreciate it," I said without enthusiasm.

He lit a cigarette.

"You don't look so good."

"I'm fine."

"You're not fine. You're quiet. You never go out. You're sad."

"Maybe a little."

"Understandable, my man. You've got to get out. I've been trying to tell you."

The waitress brought coffee.

"Thanks, doll," Mark said. "Here's the thing."

"What's that?"

He leaned across the table and cupped a conspiratorial hand by his mouth.

"The Secretary at the dealership." He looked around to make certain no one heard. "Her name's Harmony. Young. Built. And adventurous."

"You're married," I reminded him.

"Hey. I pay the bills. She sleeps all day. I get to play. Anyhow, Harmony's up for a threesome."

"A threesome?"

"You know, ménage a trois. You, me, and the beauty."

"Mark, I'm married."

"It's no problem. She's married. I'm married. We're all married. Wild gal. You'll like her. I guarantee it."

I hesitated.

"Think on it. It's there for the taking."

The waitress brought our sandwiches, and we ate. The ceremony of eating had become ponderous for me. I chewed without tasting, swallowed without feeling full. Mark ate with relish. Gratefully, he did not comment about what I left uneaten.

When we sat back with more coffee, Mark said, "You haven't seen our house."

"I haven't been invited."

"Don't be cruel, Daniel. We all make sacrifices for the

little woman. Thing is, I miss our chess matches. I told Vivian you are my friend, and I want you to visit. See our house. Play some chess. She agreed."

"She agreed?"

"Yes. Friday night. What do you say?"

"It sounds great. What time?"

"How's about seven o'clock?"

"I'll be there."

When I told Charlene, she said, "Vivian doesn't like you."

"I know. But Mark's my friend, and this might give me a chance to get to know Vivian better."

I don't think she believed it. I'm not sure I believed it, but it felt like a positive thing at a time when I needed a positive thing to happen.

When I pulled up to the curb, Vivian waited at the side of the living room window, holding a thick drape in one hand, pulling it just enough so she could check on any neighbor who might witness my arrival. I waved at her as I walked to the porch. She stared, almost invisible within the folds of the curtain.

Mark met me at the door.

"Welcome to our casa."

Vivian wore red lipstick that night and a heavy white robe over her pajamas. Even in the garb of evening, she seemed to stand in patent leather stilettos.

"Hello, Vivian," I said.

"Don't stay all night. Do not smoke in my house. And don't make any noise when you leave." As she ascended the staircase, she spoke over her shoulder to Mark. "I'm going to sleep. Don't wake me."

We waited for the bedroom door latch to click, and Mark said, "Have a seat."

I walked to the corner of their great room. Mark's chess set rested on the long rectangular table his father built. The pieces were already in place. Odette bought the chess set for him, an oak board with a smooth matt finish and exquisite cast pieces, each one intricately detailed, one side a dull silver, the other with a copper patina. It was a beautiful set, and this was the first time we had played on it since Mark stopped seeing Odette.

Mark brought a bottle of tequila and two glasses. He put them on the end of the table.

"Be right back," he said.

I sat in the chair nearest the fireplace. It had one of those electric fire boxes with artificial electric flames. The flames looked almost real.

Mark returned with a bowl of lemon slices and a dish of salt. He set those on the opposite end of the table, and said, "One more thing." He pulled a green ashtray from one pocket and a pack of cigarettes and matches from the other.

"Let the games begin," he said.

He placed one silver and one copper pawn in each hand and held his hands over the board. I touched his left hand.

"Silver," he said. "You move first."

Mark poured each of us a glass of tequila. He handed me a lemon slice. I licked my hand, touched the salt.

"Cheers," I said. "How you doing?"

"More to the point, how are you doing? How are things with Charlene?"

We drank.

"That's good," I said.

"Yeah."

He waved his long arm across the table and indicated that I should move.

I pushed King's pawn forward to e4.

"French Defense or Sicilian?" he pondered.

His strategizing at chess-playing displayed the nuances of his ability to stretch time. I drank another shot and began to relax.

"Your move."

I played the game more from remembering what each piece could do rather than from any plan. Mark, however, took this contest seriously, and he won the first game.

During the course of the game, Mark did not tell me how he was doing, nor did I answer his question regarding Charlene. We didn't need words for such concerns. We did not need to articulate the complex anxiety of faulty lives, to express in some disturbing image that which disturbed us. Our friendship had lasted through some perplexing experiences, but Mark's marriage to Vivian weakened it.

This visit, in spite of my desire otherwise, felt nervous and uncertain.

We attended to the first game with timid seriousness, neither of us wishing to disturb Vivian. During the course of that game, we finished three more shots of the tequila.

"Pour us another," I said, and he filled each glass again.

We traded colors, and Mark moved first, but not until I managed to down my shot.

"You're behind," I challenged, and pointed to my glass.

He raised his and finished it.

"Another," he said.

As Mark poured, he looked at me with the beginning of bloodshot eyes.

"You know Odette is pregnant?"

"I seem to recall that," I said. "You do realize that she and Charlene are still friends. Yes?"

"Charlene, man, you need to get away from her. For a while, I mean. You know, another woman."

When I didn't answer, he continued.

"She might have a boy," he said. "A son."

I reeled from our own child-loss, but I said nothing.

"Shit," he said, and took a long drink directly from the bottle.

We played in silence for some time, maybe ten, twelve minutes, and after several healthy swigs of my own from the bottle, I put him in check-mate.

"One to one," he said. "Time for a smoke."

We hadn't smoked, owing, I suppose, to Vivian's edict. He pulled a cigarette from his pack, placed it in his mouth, and cupped a match in the pocket of his curled fingers. He lit his and held his hand across the table so I could follow. We both exhaled with some exaggeration, and for no discernible reason, we laughed.

"Can't smoke in the house," he said, nodding his head toward the stairs.

We sat back for a few minutes, exhaling the smoke into the living area with the confidence of men on vacation.

"She's not so bad," Mark said.

I nodded.

"Really. We've all got our faults, amigo. You too, you know. You ain't perfect."

"I just whipped your ass, and if you keep insulting me, I'll do it again."

"No, really. It's not her. It's the ghost."

Mark touched the edge of his father's table. The dark oil of many hands over many years made the wood smooth, full of the oil of human hands and of history and of time. He lifted his hand away to take hold of the bottle.

"It hasn't left, you know. I can smell the thing. Mostly at night. Smells like burnt electricity."

He put out his cigarette.

"What does it want?"

"It wants something I do not have."

"What?"

"I don't know. But here's the thing. I can't let him take it, whatever it is."

"Why is that, Mark?"

"Because, it's important to me, and I can't lose it."

He lit another cigarette, took a long drag, and snubbed it out.

"It keeps me awake sometimes so I can't rest. I get up in the morning tired. You ever feel that way?"

"I do," I told him. "Sometimes I don't sleep all night, and in the morning, the sun feels more like an omen than an invitation to another day."

"Yeah, like that."

He took another long swallow and handed the bottle across the table.

I finished it.

"I'm dizzy," he said.

He slid off his chair. He got down on his knees and began brushing his hands across the carpet.

"What are you doing?"

"I think I've lost my mind. Help me find it."

I got down with him and tried my luck under the table.

"Nothing here," I reported.

"I'm drunk," Mark said.

"Yes you are," I assured him.

"Let's go outside. I need some water."

We staggered through the kitchen and out the back door.

Mark's back yard had once been beautiful. The back steps led to a brick patio. Raised flower and shrub areas lined the fences. However, it looked as if years had passed since anyone had pruned or weeded.

"Look at that moon," he said.

The white moon filled the July sky with watery shimmers, and the aura encircled it with feathery softness like early cotton.

I stared at it too, and it made me dizzy.

"You see how it dances?" Mark asked.

"It is dancing," I said.

"The ghost does that. Makes the moon dance around to startle me. Doesn't work, though. I can stop it."

Mark hoisted the end of a garden hose and plugged it into his mouth. He turned on the nozzle and gulped the flowing water, the excess spilling out onto his shirt and onto the patio. He pulled the hose from his mouth.

"Ohhhh," he said.

He turned, twisted really, like a dancer who has lost his partner. He looked again at the moon. He fell forward and vomited onto the night-gray bricks of the patio. He forced more water into his stomach, and he expunged the excess until he was out of breath.

"Shit," he said.

I walked to him and tried to lift him.

He pushed me away.

"I'll do it," he said.

He knelt erect and shook his head. I put my hand out, and he clutched it. I pulled him up.

"Daniel, I've never told you this." He wobbled a little but held his balance."I don't believe in God."

He shook his head as if clearing his thoughts."I don't believe in ghosts, either. But I have the feeling that this one has something to do with my father, so I have to pay attention. My father was important to me."

We sat again on the wet brick steps.

"I'm not a father to Vivian's kid. She won't let me. Says she's got a father. I let it go, but that sort of thing affects a man, makes him suffer. And I'll tell you, buddy, I am a man who suffers."

His speech slowed to the tempo of a drunken philosopher.

"Odette's going to have my baby. Look at me," he shouted. "I'm going to be a father." In a much quieter voice he said, "Maybe there is a God."

"I better get going," I said.

I headed toward the side gate. Mark began to follow, but suddenly, he slipped on the vomit-slippery bricks. His feet went out, and he fell backwards. He hit the back of his head and knocked himself out. Blood oozed from under his head. He did not move.

I gathered myself somewhat, returned to the living room, and phoned 911.

"Vivian," I called up the steps. "Come down here. Mark

is hurt."

When we watched the ambulance drive off, Vivian turned to me.

"Look what you've done. The siren woke the neighbors!"

Chapter 38

I visited Mark in the hospital the next day after work.

"He suffered a concussion. You may only stay a few minutes," the nurse admonished.

I walked with as much stealth as a man with a hangover could manage. I figured his head hurt worse than mine. As I neared the door, I heard Mark's voice.

"Great lunch, doll. And thanks for the ice water. Nothing like it. What's on the menu for tonight?"

He sounded like the master of ceremonies at a one-ring circus.

"You're making a lot of noise for a man with a head wound."

"Danny boy," he shouted.

"You're supposed to be hurt, resting, keeping quiet."

"Here," he said. "Take this twenty and get thee to the gift shop."

I took the twenty.

"Well?" he said.

"And what shall I retrieve from yon gift shop?"

"Two of their best cigars. We're celebrating."

"Your recovery?"

"My daughter. Odette's on the third floor. Came in this morning. Charlene brought her."

"Charlene?"

"Didn't you know?"

"I don't always know a lot of things."

"No matter," Mark said. "I'm a father." He lowered his voice. "Danny, I'm gonna be somebody's dad."

Chapter 39

Mark seemed overjoyed at the birth of his daughter, and he wanted everyone to know, even his wife.

Odette celebrated the birth more soberly, anticipating her needs. Food. Clothes. School. Parents. She did not allow Mark access to the baby. Mark wanted to name the baby Marilyn, after the movie star. Odette said she would name her daughter after she thought about it for a few days.

Charlene took no position on the quarrels between Odette and Mark. During the ensuing weeks, she subsumed the loss of her own baby within the activity of excitement that a newborn generates. She spent her days and nights at Odette's. I didn't see her. She didn't call. And, Odette asked me not to visit.

Late one night, the phone rang. It startled me awake.

"Hello?"

"Mr. Daniel Reed?"

"Who is this? Do you know what time it is?"

"This is Sergeant Yost at the Police Station. We have your wife here. Can you come for her?"

"The police station? What's going on?"

"I'll explain when you get here, sir."

I sped to the jailhouse.

"I'm Daniel Reed. I'm here for my wife."

The clerk called Sergeant Yost. He came out a side door and invited me to his office.

"Have a seat, Mr. Reed."

"Where is my wife? Tell me what's happened."

Sergeant Yost sat behind a gray metal desk. He looked at me as if I were an alien worthy of study.

"When was the last time you saw your wife, Mr. Reed?"

"Why? Is Charlene hurt? Tell me what's going on."

"We have your wife in custody, but there's a problem."

"What sort of problem? Why is she in jail?"

"When was the last time you saw your wife, sir?" he asked again.

"It's been about two weeks, no, almost three, I guess. She's been staying with a friend who had a baby."

"What's wrong with her?"

"Nothing's wrong with her. Why?"

"Father Jardine, from St. Michael's, phoned us a few hours ago. Your wife went into the Church earlier tonight."

"Yes."

"She took off her clothes and began to wash herself with the holy water. Her feet were bloody, and she wore no shoes. When Father Jardine walked in on her, he asked her what she was doing. She told him she was washing the sin marks from her body. He tried to talk to her, but she became frantic, screaming that he was the devil in black pants. He called 911."

It can't be so, I told myself. But it was so. Somehow, I knew it was so.

"Why didn't you take her to the hospital instead of to

jail?" I demanded.

"Normally we would, but technically she was trespassing. That's against the law."

"But, Sergeant . . ."

He interrupted me. "Do you want to take custody of her? Father Jardine refuses to press charges, and I must release her to a responsible party."

"Yes. Of course. I will take care of her. Can I see her?"

"It will take a little time for the paperwork. Wait here. About half an hour. You could use a cup of coffee."

He left. Someone brought coffee.

The half hour stretched to forty minutes and then to an hour, time enough for me to vacillate between the calm belief that everything would be fine and the anxiety of fear that something had seriously snapped within Charlene's connection to reality, a non-real reality along the lines of Mark's ghost.

Sergeant Yost finally returned with papers for me to sign. He escorted me to the waiting area beyond the front desk at the entry door.

When Charlene appeared, I did not recognize her. She wore a man's brown rain coat and a man's brown shoes. Her hair was matted with grime.

I rushed to her, to hold her, to save her. I hugged her. She felt skinny as a white birch, and her arms dangled. Her once vibrant eyes held no fire. They were dull, like a gloomy full moon dismayed by dark clouds.

"Charlene, what happened to you? Where have you been?"

She did not answer, and a vague despair settled upon me.

"I'm taking you home," I said.

"No," she screamed, and ran to the corner.

"We've got to go home, Charlene. We can't stay here."

"I gave him a walking statue to remember himself."

"What?"

"It's not pleasant at the Last Supper, with all those kissing the clothes. Christ told us that the politicians were too much when there aren't enough time, and we can't find the murderer."

I did not know how to hug her nor how to understand her. And, I did not know how to help her. I wanted to save her. I took her to the Emergency Room. I drove to the hospital caught in the certainty of a reality I wanted to reject, a reality I did not think I could survive. Yet I continued on, knowing I could not ease her suffering, hoping that hospitalization might bring her safely to a return to normalcy.

They put us in a waiting room and called Doctor Leonard. I asked for a cloth, and with warm water from the sink I cleaned her feet of mud and dried blood. I rinsed the cloth, wiped her feet tenderly one last time, and looked up at her.

"The mark remains," she said.

Doctor Leonard warned me against having a conversation with a person in a psychotic state, but he wasn't there, and I went ahead.

"What mark, Charlene?"

"Captain's mark. It got on me. Scrub, scrub, scrub away."

"Captain?"

"I told him to go away. I told him I was all better now. The medicine made me better. He screeched at me. Thick, hot sounds. Prickly echoes, echoes. Prick, prick. Into my brain. I asked him to stop. He made me smell words. Hard, mean words. Hate and death and bacon. And my nose tasted the words. He gagged my eyes and no tears would come out." She spoke with a scratchy throat of harsh staccato, like a file against rusty metal. "Hate and death make the brightest fire. The fire in the faces. Faces in the fire. Red and yellow faces. Long ones and short ones. Faces, smiling in fire. The faces became him. Then each face left him. One at a time. They came and they went, all the way back to Cain. And Cain became him, and he became Cain and they became fire and the fire burned. He wanted to mark me, like a painter's signature. You have no love I told him. Take your fire away. But some spilled on me."

Her sleepless eyes filled with the paranormal vision, real and terrible.

Suddenly, she looked at me.

"Do you not see, Daniel? Flesh is only a picture. The

lines of life connect in spirit. And what lingers there, behind the wall, is not all good. Only some of it is good, and you must not let the mark burn you."

Her face changed again. It seemed to shrink. Her skin turned white, not healthy with blood, rather, empty and white like a scar. Nothing that belonged to a healthy face. That moment felt like the day I stopped crying for my mother. I saw the illness in Charlene as clearly as I recognized that my mother was not coming to feed me.

I held her. I pulled her slight body against my heart, enclosed her with my arms, filled my mind with as much love for her as I could summon. I rocked her like a baby, with her transparent skin, her paranoid eyes, her tearless self. I rocked her and I held her and I wept for her.

"Charlene," I whispered. "I love you."

Finally, a nurse entered the room.

"Come with me, now," she said to Charlene. The nurse held her hand and put her other arm around Charlene's back.

"I gave him a walking statue to remember himself."

"That's nice," the nurse assured her.

"Do you know the most common roadkill in Jerusalem?"

The nurse kept walking.

"Crucifixes."

On they walked, up to the 6th floor, behind the locked doors, into the everlasting hallways of the insane.

The next day, I phoned Odette to get some information.

"Odette," I began. "What happened to Charlene? Why didn't you call me?"

"Why hasn't Charlene been back to see the baby?" she asked.

"What do you mean? She was staying with you."

"She left."

"She left? When?"

"A few days ago."

"When, Odette? When did she leave your apartment?"

"Daniel, what's wrong?"

"Odette, when did Charlene leave?"

"I don't know. Three, no, four days ago. Tell me what's going on."

"She looked terrible. Skinny. Worn out. Starving."

"Okay. She left two weeks ago, but I thought she went home."

"No, she did not come home. She got arrested yesterday. I signed her in to the hospital last night."

"You did not. How could you? She warned me. She said you planned to put her away."

"What?"

"She knows you are upset about the loss of your baby. She said you want a new wife, one that works."

"I never said anything like that."

"Oh, Daniel, I don't know what to think about you. I can't believe you sent her back to that place."

Chapter 40

I never learned where Charlene had gone or how she discovered the Church, or where she obtained the coat she wore. Her passage into the cave of her dark unconscious seemed, as I look back, merely odd. I admit that sounds shallow, but the oddities of human behavior do not always portend insanity, do they?

When I went to visit her, the nurse led me to Doctor Leonard's office.

"She's resting, Daniel, and she cannot see anyone today."

"What's happening to her?"

"She's paranoid. She's delusional. We gave her some medication, and she's beginning to rest."

"When can I see her?"

"Why don't you give her a couple of days?"

"Two days?"

"Two or three. She needs rest."

"Then I can take her home?"

"I don't advise that she go home, Daniel."

"When then? A week?"

"I wouldn't want to anticipate."

"Two weeks?"

He looked at the top of his desk. Slowly, he lifted his pipe, raised it to his lips, and struck a match. The sulfur spark rose into a yellow glow, like a miniature rocket lifting off, and he hovered the flame over the tobacco to light it. The slow, orchestrated actions reminded me of Mark's cigarette-lighting ceremony.

Doctor Leonard exhaled profoundly. He pulled the stem of the pipe from his mouth.

"Daniel, your wife is quite sick."

"I understand, Doctor. But tell me, when can she come home?"

"She can leave any time, I suppose. She is here, as we say, for observation. But I advise against it."

I sat up straight in the chair and leaned toward Doctor Leonard. Obviously, I did not yet fully grasp the complexity of our circumstances.

"Doctor?"

"Your wife is a paranoid schizophrenic. She has suffered a psychotic break from which she will never fully recover."

Doctor Leonard filled that room with a number of words that immediately impacted several areas of my brain and my nervous system. Paranoid. Schizophrenic. Never recover. Taken one at a time, out of context, these words have minimal emotional power. Together, within context, within the same sentence, within the same room, covering Charlene with their putrid decay, they made dragon-fire seem petty.

I took a Psychology in Business class, with one short chapter on mental illness. I held no deep knowledge, but I knew enough to fear the words. I don't even know why. It is as if they hold dark magic, fearsome, like the words witchcraft or inquisition.

This first clear confirmation that Charlene had manufactured her own reality did not in any way prepare me for the full brunt of the meanness of her disease.

I did not quit my job so much as I modified my hours. Mr. Ronni acted with compassion and patience when I explained my reason. Visiting hours were from 2:00 to 4:00 o'clock, and I went each day to see her. At that moment in my life I needed human understanding, and fortunately Mr. Ronni understood. He let me keep my job, even though I took off every day at 2:00, and often I focused more on missing Charlene than I did on my responsibilities at work. Frankly, without his kindness . . .

Quite honestly, I should have been fired.

Although I saw Charlene every day that first week, our visits consisted of sitting across from each other at a metal table. I drank coffee. Charlene smoked cigarettes. We did not talk. For two hours. Uncomfortable plastic chairs. At the end of the first week, on Friday, after work, after another empty visit, I sat on our living room couch, and I cried.

This solitary act, risen from the abyss of my own unconscious fears, started as a function of sadness driven by loss but developed into a form of catharsis. I cried long into that night. I continued to cry until the act became an automatic response to the loss I felt and to the empty circumstances of my life. If I missed Charlene at night, in bed, I cried for missing her. When I made coffee in the morning, and, if by habit I poured two cups, I cried. If, when leaving for work, I heard a daybreak bird song, I cried. I suppose it did not matter exactly what might happen, I needed to cry. And I cried. Perhaps this type of deep emotion, expressed in bodily display, the culmination of which overpowered common sense, served to prepare me for the eventual collapse of the once ideal life I lived and allowed for acceptance of the brutality of the life which would replace it.

My mother had a saying: It's a good life, son, if you don't weaken.

I was about to learn what she meant.

Chapter 41

At the beginning of Charlene's second week at the hospital, I arrived at 2:15. As I headed toward the entrance, I saw Odette's car in the parking lot. Before I reached the door, Odette walked out, carrying her baby in the carrier.

"Hey, Odette."

She looked away, quickened her steps, and walked past me without a word.

"Odette," I called. "Odette, hold up."

She opened her car door and secured the baby in her safety seat, all the while continuing to ignore me.

"Odette, what are you doing here? Why won't you talk to me?"

She pulled herself away from the baby and closed the door.

"Charlene told me what you did."

"What?"

"Put her in there. Locked her up. And then told them to give her those shots. Daniel, she's so hurt. How could you do those things to her?"

"Odette, I didn't do those things. They did. Doctor Leonard explained that she might confuse reality. Say things she thinks are true, but they're not."

"That's convenient."

She shook her head. "I believe Charlene. I've spoken with your Doctor Leonard, and I'm signing Charlene out of there. She's coming to live with me. And you better stay away. In a day or two, we will come to get her clothes."

I stepped out of her path and watched her drive away. I looked up to the sixth floor windows, but I could not find Charlene.

I bought a six-pack, went home, and drank the beer, which did not in any way help clarify my understanding or my judgment. Doctor Leonard warned me against self-medicating. Perhaps he knew that once the idiosyncrasies of the psyche get tangled up in the delusional invitations of alcohol, the body's chemistry begins to experiment with all the ominous possibilities of human nature, depression, anger, fear, violence, madness.

"Like Charlene?" I asked him.

"Not exactly. Her problems are systemic and unavoidable. Yours are circumstantial and controllable. However, if you continue along a path of destruction, you will eventually culminate in the successful ruination of your life."

Yeah. Yeah. Yeah.

Chapter 42

One certainty of a lived life is change. It follows, therefore, that in the midst of great change, greater change will ensue. However, neither Doctor Leonard, nor Odette, nor even the great Nostradamus could have foreseen the events that blossomed from Odette's decision to bring Charlene to her apartment.

Eight days into her move, around three o'clock in the morning, I received a call from Odette.

"Daniel. I had to do it. I'm sorry."

"What?"

"She tried to kill Ada."

"Who tried to kill Ada? Who's Ada?"

She began to cry and hung up the phone.

I drove to her apartment. A policeman stopped me before I got to her door.

"Who are you? What are you doing here?" he asked me.

"I'm Daniel Reed. I'm a friend of Odette Woodlin. She called me. Is she okay?"

"Wait here."

He went to the door. I watched him and Odette talk. Odette held the baby very close to her cheek, wrapped in a blanket, snuggled into her shoulder. Odette nodded and walked away. She left the door open, and the officer came back down the sidewalk.

"You can go in, Mr. Reed. But she's very upset. You

might want to keep your visit short."

"Okay."

I went inside and closed the door. I could feel the tension like heavy humidity before rain.

"Kitchen," Odette said.

She leaned into the corner of the counter-top, holding the baby, her eyes on the infant.

Water boiled on the stove.

"Tea," she said, and pointed to the cupboard door. "Living room," she added, and walked away.

I pulled two cups from the shelf. I put a bag of Earl Gray in each cup, filled them with water, and went to the living room.

Odette sat on the couch. I placed her tea on the side table.

I sat in the chair.

Odette finally released the baby and placed her in the carry-all on the couch next to her. She spent a long, exaggerated minute tucking the blanket just so, along the edges, and up against her innocent, infant cheeks.

The baby slept.

Odette reached for the tea, took a tentative sip, and put the cup back on the table. For a moment, she peered at the baby. She shook her head, closed her eyes. She inhaled short breaths, through her nose, uncadenced and uneasy. Tears began, and she moved off the couch, crying now in full, and hugged my head.

"Oh, Daniel, I'm so sorry."

She cried without shame, holding my head for an uncomfortable amount of time. I did not know what to make of it. When she stopped, she sniffled and returned to the couch. She found her tea and sipped.

"I couldn't stand her in that place. She told me they tortured her. She told me she was terrified. She said they would kill her."

She inhaled deeply with her mouth closed tight. She shook her head. Finally, she turned her eyes toward me.

"She didn't look right. Her eyes weren't right. They were off, like they had been taken out and put back in lopsided. And she couldn't stop smoking. One cigarette after another. It wasn't right. That Doctor Leonard said because Charlene was an adult, and there was no legal reason to hold her, I could take her out of there. All I had to do was sign some papers."

She reached over and touched the baby's blanket.

"I fixed the couch for her to sleep on."

She lifted her cup and drank.

"Earlier tonight, we ate a salad with a ripe tomato. She doted on Ada until her bedtime. Charlene went with me to put her in the bassinette in my bedroom. We returned to the living room, watched some TV. I went to bed around ten. Charlene stayed up. I heard the TV playing as I dozed off.

"At some point, the baby whimpered. She needed a

diaper change, or she was dreaming. Who knows? I opened my eyes to the sound, but she stopped, so I closed my eyes again. I didn't fall asleep, but a few seconds later, for no reason, I opened my eyes again. I saw Charlene bent over the baby. I thought she was comforting her.

"The baby lay quiet, and I smiled to myself at the thought that we composed a strange family, but a family nonetheless. Charlene walked to the other side of my bed and picked up a pillow. She must have thought I was asleep. Do you think she thought I was asleep, Daniel?"

I shrugged my shoulders. I had no answer.

"She walked back to the bassinette and began talking to Ada. 'You're my baby,' she said. 'Quiet now.' Thankfully, I turned to watch. My God, Daniel, she put the pillow over Ada, across her little body. Daniel, what possessed her?"

She shook her head, as if even she could not believe the story she was telling.

"Charlene smiled up at the ceiling. 'Yes, baby,' she said. Then she spread her hands across the top of the pillow and leaned with all her might into the bed.

"I shouted, 'What are you doing?' Charlene pushed the smothering pillow with all her strength, singing in a quiet voice, 'Hush, little baby, don't you cry.' I leaped from the bed and lunged at her. I pulled one of her arms away from the bassinette. I called to her. 'Stop. What are you doing?' 'The Captain wants our twins,' she told me, and she leaned back toward Ada. I pushed her, hard, and she backed away.

She looked at me, her eyes full of surprise. 'What's wrong, Odette?' 'Get out of this room,' I told her. 'Give me the baby,' she said, but her voice was strange, like something had torn inside her and spit bubbles filled her words. 'She belongs to him now. He took my other one to make me lonely, but he needs both of them. She wants to join her sister.'

"I lifted Ada from the bed and held her with both of my arms. The excitement startled her. I comforted her as best I could, but I could hardly breathe, hardly think. I was mad with instinct. 'You tried to kill my baby,' I screamed, and Ada began to cry. Charlene smiled at Ada, and she ignored me. I managed to force Charlene toward the door, and I backed her down the hall into the living room. 'Sit down,' I said, but Charlene stood. I pushed her on the shoulder. 'Sit,' I said. Suddenly, obedient and compliant, she sat on the couch, folded her hands, and stared intently at the floor."

Odette lifted her cup to drink, but it was empty. She looked at me with a complex of guilt and anger in her face.

"I sent her back there, Daniel. I don't know if she belongs there, maybe she does. I don't know. But she tried to kill my baby."

"It's alright, Odette. I'll go to her. I'll take care of her."

She did not say any more. After a time of silence, I rose.

"I'll check on you in a few days."

She held the empty teacup in both hands and watched her baby.

Chapter 43

On my first visit after Odette returned her to the hospital, Charlene seemed upset. She smoked a cigarette, pulling it away from her lips and exhaling immediately, a jerky, uncoordinated effort. She looked like an explorer who awoke to discover herself in an inaccessible country.

"Hi, Honey," I said.

"Why are you here?"

"I've come to see you."

"You hate me."

"Don't talk like that. I love you."

"Take me home."

"I can't."

"You hate me."

She continued to smoke, exhaling rapid exhaust from her mouth and her nose. She would not look at me. She gazed straight ahead with what I can only describe as an angry vagueness in her eyes.

"Do you know the most popular roadkill in Arizona?" Charlene asked.

"No."

"Scorpions. How about Georgia?"

"No."

"Opossums."

"If you were a state," she said, "you would be a snake. Be gone, Satan."

She turned one-half a turn away from me and lit another smoke so that she held two burning cigarettes between her fingers, one in each hand.

"You can't escape your roadkill," she said. "Virginia? Brown rabbit. Massachusetts? Brown clams. Hawaii? Brown dolphins. Florida? I don't know Florida. Captain has kept that information from me because there are too many spies in Florida."

I walked to the exit door, and she continued addressing her cigarettes, accumulating an ongoing directory of state-identified roadkill. Doctor Leonard warned me not to argue with her. But sometimes I wanted to argue, to discuss, to halt the growing distance between us, between our words, between our worlds.

"Why can't I argue?" I wanted to know.

"You can't argue with a crazy person," Doctor Leonard explained.

I could not conceive of Charlene as a crazy person. Crazy felt unbalanced, frightening, full of disturbances I did not want to encounter, like ghosts or bankruptcy. I could get a hold of ideas like woman or friend or wife. These motifs fit my understanding. They behaved within a realm of reasonableness I trusted.

To be honest, that visit with Charlene hurt me.

"How could she say such a thing to me?"

"I've been trying to tell you, Daniel. Your wife is sick, and the illness has taken her away from you. Look at this."

He lifted some fragments of paper from the center drawer of his desk. They were torn and wrinkled. He arranged them so the torn ends matched, like an odd paper puzzle.

"What do you make of this?" he asked me.

"A strange Rorschach test."

Doctor Leonard looked disapprovingly at me. He lifted his pipe and lit it. The gentle aroma and thick smoke added to his somber demeanor.

"This is a note written by Charlene."

"There's no writing on it."

"That's a very interesting observation, Daniel. Would you care to say more?"

I admired Doctor Leonard's consistency. He never seemed to adventure outside his psychiatrist character.

"No thanks," I said. "You already analyze me with more regularity than I approve."

"I see."

"What is it?"

"This note from Charlene contains no words, no letters. Yet, it is her serious attempt to communicate."

"I don't get it," I admitted.

"I will try to explain. This wrinkled paper holds great significance for Charlene. She attempted to express her despair. She tried to share that with you."

"With me?"

He set his pipe in the ashtray.

"When I met with her this morning, she appeared quite angry."

"Why?"

"Because she held this secret message, unreadable to us, but clear and meaningful to her. The paper was hidden in her pocket, and she expected you to read it. Of course, you were not present, and I had no idea she held a secret message in her pocket."

"Of course."

Doctor Leonard squinted his displeasure of my ironic imposition, and he re-lit his pipe.

"Nevertheless," he continued, "in the middle of our session, she rose abruptly from that chair you're sitting in and pulled the message from her pocket. She tore the paper and wrinkled the pieces in agitation. Then, she threw these scraps on my desk. She went to the door. But before she left, she said, 'Since you refuse to discuss this, obviously you can't help me because you and he are in this together.'"

"What did she mean?"

"As I indicated, it's a coded message that attempts to explain her despair. For you, it means that she can no longer communicate to you. At least not the way most of us communicate. She lives in her own world. And that means you can no longer communicate with her."

"Does she make sense to you? Do you understand her world?"

"I can interpret her symbols, yes."

"Then I can learn, too."

"That's not really possible."

"Why?"

"I'm a trained psychologist."

"Well, I'm a husband."

"Really, Mr. Reed, what does a husband know?"

Chapter 44

A few days later, I went to check in with Odette. She let me into the apartment without a word. Boxes of clothes and pictures wrapped in newspaper rested on the floor, orderly and sad.

"Sit down," she called.

I moved some magazines from the seat of the chair and sat down. Odette brought a cup of coffee and placed it on the table for me. She guarded the baby in the carry-all. She returned to the kitchen and brought a second cup of coffee for herself. She placed the baby on the couch next to her so she could touch her while we talked.

"I've met with Doctor Leonard," I began.

"Charlene is the best friend I ever had. And I will always love her."

She sipped her coffee.

"But, Daniel, she tried to kill . . ."

She looked at her child.

"I named her after my mother, you know. Ada."

"I don't know much about your family."

She nodded, still looking at the baby.

"I didn't want to leave home. I was scared. Mama said I have the wanderlust in my blood. She's right, I guess. I thought California could satisfy some itch I had about a better life. A different life. I don't know. I do like the cities, and I love the mountains. But there are mountains in

Wyoming, too, and the lights of California can blind. The people here do not know one another. There is too much fear and too much selfishness. That's why I love Charlene. She's not like that. She's tender and fragile. Too fragile, I guess."

"Where are you from?"

She pulled her legs onto the cushion and leaned back.

"We have a ranch just outside of Alcova, Wyoming."

"I never heard of it."

"Near Casper," she said. "The red cliffs, ragged and eroded like old faces. A constant wind across the plain. I remember them now like a moving thought that never sleeps. Oh, Daniel, since I've been here, no one in my family has suffered like me. But I don't want that for Ada. I'm taking my baby home where we will be safe and where people will love us. I can already smell the spring lavender. I can see the open sky and our house in a wilderness of space with the horizon far away. I'm going home."

She rocked gently, her eyes closed, her white fingers tight around the coffee cup. I stood and said good bye.

"Daniel, move on. I love Charlene and I love Mark, but I let them go. I will store the good memories. Do the same, Daniel. Let her go."

I never saw her again.

Chapter 45

Learning new things is difficult. Learning new things one does not really want to learn is more difficult. The next few months do not invite easy scrutiny. In fact, looking closely still hurts. An injured animal retreats to its cave and licks its wounds to allow time and chemistry to heal them. Humans devise as many methods to heal as there are individual wounds.

Charlene suffered a total psychotic break, what Doctor Leonard described as "a loss of meaningfulness, a loss of purpose, and an acceptance of despair." I could not, would not, accept her loss. I had not yet uncovered the lesson of permission. Instead, I used my daily energy to combat Charlene's dying emotions, a loss of vitality not unlike physical death, except she did not die. To express this more accurately, her body did not die, but her perception of comprehendible reality did. To make up for that loss, she created an alternate world.

Doctor Leonard explained this phenomenon as "the psyche's loss of ability to integrate internal and external reality."

"What does that mean?" I asked him.

"Charlene, at this moment in time, is living a life the reality of which exists only in her mind, and this new world she has created denies her past as well as her present."

Some ideas in psychology seem like listening to a rock

formation explain how it achieved its ability to hold still.

Because Charlene committed a violent act, the state required Doctor Leonard to send her for long term care to the state institution in Napa. Immediately, they increased her dosage of Thorazine.

Because of laws and paperwork and the general lack of effort on the part of bureaucratic lethargy, it took more than a week before she was settled and I could see her.

The hospital grounds looked like a well-kept home with a great, expansive lawn within which the staff had chained small wooden benches to some of the shade trees. The main building looked haunted, a gloomy, multi-storied, Gothic prison with bars across each window and locks on all the doors. When they finally allowed me entrance, a male nurse escorted me down the hall. One woman, incontinent, crawled along the floor, next to the wall, dragging her dirty skirt, leaving a trail. One thin man with an aquiline nose leaned against a barred window counting the three longest fingers of his left hand, one at a time, again and again. One gray-haired man gripped his hat with both hands and squeezed it repeatedly. All revealed eyes caught in the doldrums of antipsychotic Nirvana and wild with the inferno of collapsed reality.

In the midst of this cruel collection of misery, he pointed to Charlene sitting in a chair by a column in the middle of a large, square room. I did not recognize her from afar. Her already frail body looked thinner. She would not talk. She smoked with odd, difficult gestures as if her muscles were on a string.

I sat with her for half an hour, but I could tolerate the discomfort no longer, as if a glass dome had been lowered, and within it the soundless throb of a vacuum pounded in my ears.

I went to Doctor Leonard.

"She doesn't look right."

"What do you mean?"

"She's lost more weight. She wouldn't talk. And her body movements were strange. The way she smokes, for instance."

"Yes?"

"Her hand is stiff, like this." I held my hand up with all the fingers stretched out like a first grader who is going to trace his hand print for a Mother's Day card. "Then she puts the cigarette in her mouth, inhales and exhales. Real quick, like this." I showed him. "She's all stiff. Her movements look mechanical not muscular. It's like she isn't thinking about anything, only reacting."

"That's not exactly accurate, but it's close."

"What do you mean?"

"Thorazine has some side effects."

"Like what?"

"We have names like affective flattening, avolition, tardive dyskinesia. Sometimes the muscles relax too much, and, as you say, gestures can appear stiff. Sometimes patients develop a twitch around the eyes or the lips."

"I don't care what you call them. Do they go away?"

"Some can be permanent."

"That doesn't seem good."

"The alternatives are worse. The drugs help control her symptoms."

"Will they heal her?"

"I wouldn't say healed."

"Not healed?"

"No."

"I don't see how she's better."

"Would you rather she remain in a state of panic, communicating with her Captain, terrorized by her daemons?"

"No," I admitted. "I don't want to see her like that. But I do not want to see her like she is, either."

"It's better."

"It might be better, but I don't like it. I want my wife back. Like she was. I want the woman I love to come home to me."

Doctor Leonard allowed the pipe smoke to circle above us like a gathering nimbus of unpleasant information.

"Daniel," he said very softly, "a schizophrenic break as severe as Charlene's permanently damages the personality. The woman you married does not exist anymore."

"I don't believe it."

I jumped from the chair. I paced the confines of the

office.

"No." I leaned on the front of the desk. "She's going to get well. I'm going to make her well."

The session ended. I didn't want to talk anymore. Maybe never again. I just wanted to go to my room to make a space for Charlene and me. A safe place. A place where we would not hurt anymore.

Charlene did not come home, of course, and I needed other visits to gain some acclimation. But it took time. My second visit devastated me.

Charlene moved with less catatonic-like misery, and she did appear less agitated, although the exaggerated body movements remained. We went to a table, and I sat across from her.

"How are you, Honey?"

She held her cigarette and smoked. She did make brief eye contact, but she looked past me quickly and again stared as if I did not exist.

"Charlene, will you talk to me? Please?"

I had a styrofoam cup of black coffee, and I sipped at it, little sips, glancing over the top to see if any change would come to her. None did. We sat in silence, listening to the chatter and moans and an occasional scream from one of the other patients. But Charlene did not chatter, nor moan, nor scream. I finished the coffee, bitter, lukewarm, grinds in the last mouthful.

"Well," I said, "I guess I'll go."

I stood.

Charlene continued her fixation on the cigarette filter, which had burnt and smelled like an unchanged diaper.

I walked around the table and bent to kiss her on the cheek. As I did, she spoke.

"You did this to me."

"What?"

"Put this sickness on me. It's not mine. It's yours. Take it away."

"I don't know how to take it away. I would if I could."

"You let them take our furniture. You let them take our baby. You let them take me. It's all your fault."

I wanted her well. I wanted to help. Maybe if I assumed blame I could restore her, and instantaneously, guilt overwhelmed my thought process.

"Did I drive her mad? Is her illness my fault?" I asked Doctor Leonard.

"It's possible, but not likely."

"It's possible?"

"As anything is possible. But not likely."

"Please, Doctor. Tell me what happened to Charlene."

"I don't know, Daniel. No one knows."

"But she's right," I said. "We lost our baby. We lost our furniture. I lost the bar, and we are bankrupt. Could all these cause a schizophrenic break?"

"Yes. Any dramatic event might become a trigger."

"Oh, God."

"Of course," he continued, "many people do survive tragedy. You yourself have survived these same experiences you name."

For some reason, I did not want to hear that. It sounded logical, but at the same time unfair, as if it were an excuse instead of an observation. Why should I be well and not Charlene?

"Is all your knowledge limited to possibility only?"

He puffed quietly on his pipe.

"What causes schizophrenia?" I asked in frustration.

"There are many theories. Biological predisposition, inappropriate family nurturing, cultural complexities, in-uterus trauma, drugs, alcohol, some of these, all of these, one of these. Acute stress, as we've said. None of these, something unknown."

"It's impossible."

"That is correct. Try to imagine this. Think of our psychic health, our psyche if you will, as a round stone wheel. Picture it rolling along through all of the innumerable experiences of life. Let us say that one of the experiences bumped into the wheel and chipped it just a little. Then some time later, some different occurrence, or stimuli, bangs into that chipped area, just a little, but enough to enlarge the chip. Two such events might be enough, maybe a certain personality needs more, but eventually the chip becomes enough of a burden to send the wheel out of round, out of balance. When the wheel wobbles, or if you prefer, when the psyche wobbles, we lose touch with conventional reality. We see things, hear things, that others do not. We create fears that have no observable cause. We lose our minds. If you further consider that our five senses, and the activities of the conscious and the unconscious collectively accumulate billions of stimuli every year, do you think you could go back in Charlene's life and pick out that one instant when her wheel was first chipped?"

They entailed the most words I think he ever said to me at one time, but they struck with fierce acuity. If his analogy were accurate, who could ever say what drove Charlene to madness. I needed to think. I felt completely disoriented. I could not absorb newly transfigured reality, complex medical terminology, marital alienation, and the isolation of rejection all at once. One simply does not learn such complexity in business school. Even with comprehension, acceptance of a new understanding of reality takes time. I learned a difficult truth – hell is knowing that what you don't believe, you must believe.

On one visit, Charlene claimed that I was stealing her mail. Her proof included the fact that she had received no letters from the members of her sixth grade grammar school class.

On another visit, she insisted that Doctor Leonard had conspired with the head nurse to poison her food. Her proof for that included the fact that on Wednesday night they had mashed potatoes with dinner instead of green peas.

At one meeting, although her voice sounded like a very old woman, she whispered in my ear, "Sometimes I feel sane."

Over many months, I began an osmosis of forbearance. Gradually, I tolerated Charlene's enumeration of state road kill. I inured to her accusations. I even managed to hold in abeyance my desires for her love and for her affection.

I do not hold as valid the principle that a schizophrenic mind suffers alone. She might live in her own made-up world, but she did not suffer alone. I suffered with her. I made that choice.

Doctor Leonard encouraged me to stop my visits, to move on with my life.

"The woman you married is gone," he told me, "and she will never return. You are wasting your energies on a lost cause."

"You sound as if there is no hope."

"Once you accept that, life gets easier."

"Without hope, there is only despair."

"That is the true human condition. And once you accept that, the pain and losses of life can no longer destroy your psychological equilibrium."

"That's crazy."

"Fighting it is crazy."

"Well, I'm fighting it."

"You must accept hopelessness, Daniel, before you can be healed."

"I thought Charlene is the sick one."

"She is lost, but you can be saved."

"I've got enough hope for both of us."

He was, in some respects, a man of kindness, but science had dulled his wisdom.

"Doctor Leonard," I said, "I cannot quit. Charlene and I are married."

"Have you not thought of divorce?"

"Yes. I have thought about it, but I'm not divorcing my wife. I will honor our vows."

"What vows? They are relics. They have no substance in this modern world, Daniel. Be reasonable."

"I was reasonable when I married her. I admit I was nervous. But nervous does not mean unconscious. I meant every word I spoke. So did Charlene."

"How do you know this?"

"We promised to accept one another for richer and for poorer. I filed bankruptcy. You can't get any poorer than that. Charlene did not divorce me."

His pipe worked smoke plumes like a train straining uphill.

"And, Doctor Leonard, we promised to love and to cherish one another in sickness and in health. We didn't exclude any illnesses. We didn't write footnotes. These are the conditions of our life. Everybody endures their life conditions and then they die. We will endure together. Circumstances are merely the things we endure."

"What, exactly, do you think you have that is of any value, any strength, to allow this endurance?"

"We have memory and daily contact."

"Her memory differs from yours."

"Isn't that true of everyone?"

"She does not recognize you."

"Sure she does."

"Not you. Not who you are. She has allied you with her Captain. You are now part of the conspiracy of her delusional terror."

"I know better."

"She does not."

"The one who knows the truth must not give up."

"You both know truth as you each perceive it. Who can say who is right, who is wrong?"

"Not right or wrong, Doctor. Well or ill, hurting or not hurting."

"Well and ill are relative terms, and can you truly say you too are not hurting?"

Of course, I hurt. I knew the tremors of anguish that terrorized my body in the dark hours. But I meant hurting in a different way. Charlene hurt as one alone, unable to explain her isolation, unable to share it. Yes, I, too, suffered alone, as each one suffers alone, but I was aware of it. I recognized the brutality of it, and I accepted the lifelong necessity of it. It is the fee charged for the everlasting connection of a man and a woman who share the promise encapsulated within "till death do us part."

Mark, in his philosophy, was also wrong. It is not about the money, but it is about the cost.

Chapter 46

One does not bring about meaningful change by wishing. It occurs through the gradual embellishment of attitude and the application of will to action. Learning to accept Charlene's new reality helped me to step away from the everyday monotony of wealth-quest in order that I might organize my priorities from the depth of my spirit rather than by the summation of our bank accounts.

I had many conversations with myself and with my Lord, a fact I failed to confide to Doctor Leonard. No telling how he might interpret such auditory practices.

One evening as I sat on our couch, I fought to discover some clear way to explain Charlene to myself. I felt that I had come near to her lost soul at the hospital, but I had not understood her. I needed to understand, and I wanted to bring my sensations to words. Something clever like how Mark Twain said that the difference between the right word and the almost right word is the difference between lightning and the lightning bug. I think that's so clever, you know? Lightning is a spectacular display of nature's electrical power. It can light a storm-black sky and back-light a forest and turn the view into a momentary vision of eerie spirits. It can flash out from a pugnacious cloud and run a jagged bolt straight into the center of the earth.

On the other hand, the humble lightning bug has no such majesty. Its feeble spark is limited to the imagination of a child, and the light it generates can't hold a candle to lightning.

Then I thought about a childhood event of my own when I saw hundreds of lightning specs flashing in a small clearing encircled by blue spruce trees. I imagined them as tiny fairies flitting around the area comforting pine needles and blades of wild grass. I captured about twenty of those lightning bugs in a mason jar. I held them under my sheet that night, and they never complained. All night long they used up their pale yellow electricity to provide a delicate security of light in the dark fright of my cloth-made cave.

Then I remembered that once I watched lightning strike a mid-life oak tree. I was driving up toward Shasta, and a storm rolled over the hills. The lightning bolt's jagged line of approach arched directly across the roadway and speared the central trunk of the tree with a sizzling sound that hissed so loud I heard it with the windows closed. I stopped to watch the startling white flash penetrate the tree, and I noticed a tiny plume of smoke rush forth from the point of impact. At the same time, the larger of two main branches cracked, and I could hear the awful snap of its fractured wood as it fell, almost in slow motion, its leaves flopping against the shudder of descent. The great arm of the tree broke, and crashing against the trunk, it bounced onto the ground. Immediately, an orange flicker burst forth from the wound, and fire erupted. The delicious smell of freshly cut green wood mingled with the muddy smell of the storm as the heart of the tree burned.

I shook my head at the fusing of these two memories. Where were they leading me? I struggled to find a way to understand insanity the way Charlene experienced insanity by comparing two light-mysteries of nature.

When someone you love goes away and you miss that person; you try to understand what is happening to both of you. At least I did.

I remembered reading this novel about the war. These Army guys found their buddy tied to a tree in the jungle. He was in a sitting position, his legs straight in front of him on the ground. His arms were cinched above his head, and his hands were tied together. He was naked. The skin had been peeled off his torso, and his penis was stuck in his mouth.

I tried to picture in my mind what such a discovery would look like, feel like.

They said he was tied with three ropes, one around his hands holding his arms up, one around his neck, and one around his stomach. The strips of skin had begun to dry and shrivel, and bugs, flies, and ants had already taken to the carcass.

I wondered what it must have been like to experience such treatment.

They said his eyes were closed when they found him, but they must have been open while he was alive. When the man who killed him began to cut the first strip of skin, didn't he say, hey, wait a minute, you can't do that. You have to leave my skin where it is.

I tried to imagine the physical sensation.

Feeling the exquisitely sharpened blade slice along his neck, across his shoulders, down his chest. Listening to the cloth-soft tearing as the skin pulled away. The extraordinary vinegar-burn as the air touched muscles that had never touched air. What terror, knowing that this isolated moment constituted the hideous culmination of his life.

I thought how could one human being do such a thing to another human being? What would drive someone?

I thought about the other soldier.

Was he afraid? Did some member of his family suffer such abomination? His mother? His father? His wife? Did the beastly behavior of another human being compel him to depravity?

The cutting of the penis, was that tribal? By that gesture, did he think he would remove the manhood of his enemy? Or perhaps take his manhood and add it to his own?

And the dead soldier, before he died, did he forgive his enemy? Did he curse him to a life of continued brutality?

If the situation were reversed, would he have killed in like manner? If so, would his enemy have forgiven him?

I grew dizzy with this perplexity of perversion. This thinking was even more puzzling than the lightning and the lightning bug, and yet, in a strange, crazy way, it began to make sense. I decided to talk it through with Doctor

Leonard.

I explained how a thing can appear one way, and, under a different perspective, it can appear contrary, and upon further reflection, both perceptions can appear simultaneously similar and dissimilar.

"Daniel," he said, "you are making untidy ideas. These are morbid thoughts. Unfit for you."

I could tell he was serious because he forced billows of floating discharges from the side of his mouth without removing the pipe from his teeth.

"You're right," I said. "But endless violence overwhelms my thinking. And no matter what approach I take to try to understand human nature, I discover violence and meanness in everyday events."

"What do you mean?"

"When I think about the beauty of nature, for example, the lightning and the lightning bug, I realize not many people actually live in the wild of nature because it is far too violent and uncaring. When I think about war, instead of beauty, you know, peace and freedom and so on, the reality of it reveals that wars never stop, and soldiers are taught to die well. Don't you see? We're not taught to live well. We're taught to die well. We can't live with nature in peace, and we can't live with people in peace."

"Daniel, you must reign in your imagination or you will endanger your own stability."

"Doctor Leonard, listen to me. I look at people, how

they treat one another, the grocer who cheats the customer, the retailer who buys from sweat shops, the oil company that destroys the environment. The greed. The meanness."

Doctor Leonard's thumb and finger pressed against the bowl of his pipe. He spoke slowly.

"This talk, this thinking, it will drive you crazy."

"That's my point exactly!" I said. "You told me that an insane person doesn't like his or her reality. Like Charlene. Maybe she went crazy on purpose. Maybe she looked at the pain people bring to one another as a consequence of base human nature, magnified by her treatment as a child, magnified again by the poignancy of her own traumas, and she's so sensitive that she could endure no more. When she reached that point, maybe at that exact moment, she left this world and she went to a safer place, like I did under the covers of my bed with the fire flies. Maybe she's not the crazy one, Doctor Leonard."

"Who then, Daniel? You and me?"

"Are we?"

"No."

"A bullet is less cruel than torture, but it kills nonetheless. If we condone cruelty, if we act with cruelty, are we animals?"

"Not animals. Survivors."

"And Charlene?"

"Do not continue to carry Charlene."

"I'm just trying to understand her. If I understand her, I

can forgive her, and if I can forgive her, I will always have hope."

"There is no hope."

"She's fragile. Delicate."

"She cannot come back to you."

"Then I can go to her."

"No."

"Call me crazy, but I love her."

"Love cannot save her."

His pipe had gone out, and he re-set his forearm on the desk. He curled his finger around the pipe bowl, and the stem pointed away from him. He looked past me, toward the wall, but not at it. Small seconds of time drifted like smoke into the emptiness of the silence. Doctor Leonard breathed inaudibly through his nose. His eyes did not move. Then quietly, like the soft approach of a field mouse, he whispered.

"My mother escaped with me when I was an infant. My father died at Treblinka in Poland."

The sun rays behind the window glinted up and down, but Doctor Leonard did not notice, and the emptiness of the moment filled the room with leaden anguish.

"I will never forgive them. Father murdered. Mother lost to grief. No one cares about the suffering I have known."

His arm did not move, and his eyes remained fixated on the past. He barely breathed.

I lifted myself from the chair, my hands tight against the armrests, leaning on my toes like someone trying not to wake a sleeping baby.

I walked out the door and pulled it closed softly.

Chapter 47

I missed Charlene more as each day passed. Even so, I began to learn how to accept the loss her illness demanded. I made progressive adjustments in my ability to pattern my choices within the circumference of that illness.

I needed a fall coat. The Lambstock Company had an outlet store where they sold last year's inventory at a discount. They were a small company, but their product was good, and they were having a sale. The outlet store was located in a small metal building about three miles out of town near the concrete plant. It had a gravel parking lot. Inside, hundreds of coats hung on wooden racks. I walked around, touching wool and cotton, shiny leather and soft felt.

Halfway down one of the aisles, I found a sporty looking, green early fall or late spring coat with yellow rope trim around the collar and the cuffs. I tried it on. It fit perfectly, plenty of shoulder room and snug around the stomach. I looked in the mirror, admiring the fit, when suddenly I felt Charlene's disapproving stare. I could see her nodding in the negative. Too loud. Makes you look too young. Attracts attention to you. I put it back on the hanger and hooked the neck of the hanger over the bar.

I returned to the lighter-weight winter coats. I'd seen a brown one I was sure Charlene would pick out for me. I pushed my arms through the sleeves and cinched it tight across the chest. Brown, ordinary, non-descript. Exactly what she'd approve. I looked in the direction of the green coat with the yellow trim and the athletic cut. Then I folded the brown cloth coat over my arm and walked to the cash register.

I put the coat on the counter, and in an unbidden moment of courage, I told the check-out girl to hold off a minute.

I walked to the green coat.

"Charlene," I thought, "I really like this coat. I know you would not want me to buy it if you were here. But you're not here, are you? Something's happened to you that I don't understand. I don't understand this decision either, but I want this coat. Not the brown one."

Toward the end I was talking out loud, and a short woman with red hair grabbed her son and rushed him to a different aisle.

"I'm sorry," I said. But not to the customer, to Charlene. And I was sorry, too, because somehow I knew that by this simple act of independence, I changed our relationship. By this act, I admitted that Charlene was really sick, and that I had to carry on in the manner of a man married to a woman who lived in an institution with barred windows.

I carried the green coat to the check-out counter.

"This one," I said.

She began to put it in a bag.

"I don't need that," I said. "I'll wear it."

I stretched my arms into the coat and squeezed it tight around me. I never felt more certain of my love for Charlene and simultaneously more independent of the need for her to return it.

That decision, and the action of it, established the impetus for our life-long struggle. I gave Charlene permission to live whatever reality she chose in order to survive the tumultuous perils of her fears. No judgments. Her choices. Sane, insane, understandable, incomprehensible, didn't matter. Her freedom. Her consequences.

The earth trembled upon its axis at that moment, recognizing the universal disturbance I caused, and in response, something miraculous happened to me. I realized that I could grant such permission to myself. That I could choose such power, and no chains, no laws, no insanity prevented such a choice. With some trepidation, I granted it, bestowed upon myself the knighthood of free will. I decided that I too choose the freedom to live whatever reality I need in order to survive the perils within the metamorphosis of my life. I could make my own happiness just as Charlene had made her own world.

Although I chose to remain devoted to Charlene, I did not desire the terror and isolation that the abandonment of cultural security provides. I also refused Doctor Leonard's abandonment of hope, for it dismisses the possibility of intentional change.

Nevertheless, on my next visit to Charlene, I stopped off

to model the coat for Doctor Leonard. He nodded behind a pungent cloud of cherry tobacco smoke.

"This is a good sign," he said. "By your actions you have chosen to abandon an unreasonable hope."

Frankly, I was close to abandoning my sessions with Doctor Leonard.

"I will not abandon hope," I told him. "I bought a coat as a man independent of the need for approval. Well," I cautioned, "that's not quite accurate. I still want Charlene's approval, but I simply realized I can live without it."

Doctor Leonard didn't see it my way.

"You're splitting psychological hairs," he said. "You've got to stop thinking of her as your wife!"

"Your pipe went out," I told him, and ended the session.

When I left Doctor Leonard, I decided to go for ice cream before heading over to see Charlene. I would have preferred the comfort of human compassion, a gentle hand on mine, or something intimate and tender like a hug or a kiss, but I settled for rocky road ice cream.

The inside of the store glared with the sharp white brightness of florescent tubes. Two people stood in line ahead of me, and almost immediately several boisterous adolescents queued behind me. The teenagers, full of energy, laughed and teased each other, and I thought how it would be to have no memories so that I could feel free to laugh. I did not have that luxury. I did, however, have a new, green coat.

A young girl worked the counter.

"What'll you have?" she asked.

"Do you have rocky road?"

"One scoop or two?"

"One," I said.

"Cup or cone?"

"Cone," I told her.

"Regular or waffle?"

"Waffle," I decided.

"Vanilla or cinnamon?"

"I just want a scoop of rocky road ice cream," I told her.

"What's the hold up?" one of the kids behind me asked.

"Vanilla or cinnamon?" the counter girl asked again without looking at me.

"Vanilla," I said.

"Medium or large?"

"Medium, please."

"Medium gets two scoops," she said. "You want both of them chocolate?"

"Chocolate? No. I want one scoop of rocky road."

"Oh," she said, "in a cup or a cone?"

"Hey, what's taking so long?" the voice behind asked.

"In a cone," I said.

She handed me a cardboard cup with one scoop of chocolate ice cream in it and a small, blue plastic spoon in a cellophane wrapper. I went outside under the shade of the mansard. The strangeness of the experience made me realize that Charlene was right about something. Life had grown complicated. She might be crazy, but she had her finger on the pulse of things. Although I did not succeed in getting my ideal, a scoop of rocky road in a vanilla flavored waffle cone, I did get ice cream. What is life, after all, if not a series of surprisingly entertaining compromises? And compromise comes in different flavors.

When I arrived back at the hospital, I found Charlene standing near a window. She held one arm with the other and smoked her cigarette with that uncoordinated tardive dyskinesia stiffness of limbs. I went to her and looked over her shoulder out the window at the smoke gray clouds framed within iron bars.

"Hi, Honey."

She exhaled smoke and looked at me, her eyes dull but not exactly inert. She had gained weight, another side effect of the psychotropics. However, without exercise, the weight made her look pudgy and flabby.

"I had a scoop of ice cream today."

"Why? You hate ice cream."

"I don't hate ice cream. I like ice cream."

"The most common roadkill in Alaska is rocky road ice cream," she informed me.

I walked to the seating area and hung my new jacket across the back of a chair. I picked up a copy of a sports magazine and sat down. The sun broke through the clouds, and penetrated the window, binding Charlene in the soft shadows of the iron bars. The sun made her haggard face appear momentarily brighter around the cheeks.

She walked over and sat in the chair across from me.

"I like your coat," she said.

Chapter 48

Our visits remained unspectacular, but I made them consistently. We met in the lounge. The patients didn't talk much, so in spite of the large numbers gathered in the vast cavern, the noise level was low, except during those times when one of the patients exhibited excessive uneasiness or loss of control. Normally, I read a magazine, and Charlene smoked cigarettes, sometimes sitting across from me, sometimes standing behind me, and sometimes next to her favorite barred window blowing smoke through the bars, watching it swirl against the glass. We drank cups of coffee from small Styrofoam cups filled from the two endless stainless steel coffee makers set up on a table along the wall near the door.

She hardly ever looked me in the eye. In fact, she rarely looked anyone in the eye. Over time, she gained more weight, the drugs generally kept her anxiety under control, and occasionally we talked.

Since our future was limited by Charlene's condition and her place of residence, our discussions rarely exceeded generalities. We didn't have much to say about plans for the future for example. She would talk about something she saw on television, a news item, or an actress she thought she recognized. Sometimes she told me about one of the patients, something she intuited; something no one else saw. I never knew whether her psychological observations were delusional or whether she somehow managed to keep her remarkable ability to read people.

Mostly, I told her about my work and sometimes about what I had for breakfast.

One sunny day, we walked around the grounds. She had selected one of the benches under the protection of a shade tree as a safe place to talk. I mentioned that I watched birds fly around at the park.

"I like hummingbirds because they are gentle," she told me. Then in a rare gesture, she looked me right in the eyes. "They are not allowed to be road kill," she insisted.

She entwined her fingers and squeezed them together very tight, and she continued to look at me.

"I know I'm crazy," she said. "Daniel, there's no suffering so awful. To lose your mind and know you will never find it. It's the very worst thing that can happen to you."

Chapter 49

I returned to school at night and finished my business degree. Mr. Ronni likes me, and I like the work and the people I work with. I bought a house outside of town. It has a small redwood deck and a big back yard with sycamore trees. It is far enough from the city to enjoy the little wonders of nature, a doe and her fawn, a woodpecker rattling a tree. I hung three hummingbird feeders, one for Charlene, one for Ella, and one for me.

One Friday morning, before I left for work, I received a call from Doctor Leonard.

"Daniel," he began, "I am sorry to tell you that Charlene passed during the night from tumors in her lungs. Her smoking."

He paused a moment, then continued.

"She was comfortable," he assured me. "A nurse sat with her at the end."

I did not speak.

"Daniel, are you all right?"

"Yes," I said. "Yes. I'll be okay."

"They will cremate the body this afternoon. You may pick up the ashes tomorrow."

"Okay," I said, and hung up.

Dead.

I do not think she died from tumors. It was her heart. I think it broke. Her frail, gentle spirit finally gave way.

At long last, Charlene came to the completion of her prolonged misery.

Her end forewarned me of my own. But not in a fearful way, more as a reminder that we are here for some unknowable number of days, and then one day we are not.

Funny, though, anger and compassion seemed to meld into a fumbling demand for expression. I wanted to talk.

Instead, I wrote her a letter.

Friday, May 14th

Dear Charlene:

I'm sorry I was not with you last night, that you had to die alone with some stranger sitting in a chair next to you. We are all alone, I guess. Still, I wish I could have been there for you.

I missed you deeply all the years of your illness because you lived in some faraway place I could not reach. And I miss you now. I wonder if it's okay to tell you I still love you? That we have remained friends? I wonder if I dare to finally tell you how your illness destroyed my life and how I had to reconstruct every aspect of it new while loving you and trying to stay in love with you?

Even though I knew you were sick, I was very angry at you sometimes. Very angry.

Dear God, sometimes I was worn out with giving and not receiving. One day at a time, Doctor Leonard would say. He meant to take one day at a time to heal. He never comprehended the fact that when you left me, when you lost touch with reality, when you blamed me for your terrors, when you said you hated me – I lost my wife, my best friend, and I lost my life.

One day at a time for me meant one tiny piece of a new life discovered, analyzed, accepted, put in place. But not in order, because there was no center. I had to re-learn all things without you.

Wow. I did not know I could be so truthful to you. It's been so long since we've talked.

Maybe Doctor Leonard was right. I might have kept some things bottled up.

I can't fully accept that you are dead. We did not plan for death. I did not often like our life of separation, but I did not plan for separation by death. And, in spite of it, I want you to stay, even if you remain just out of sight but always there.

Be at peace.
All my love,

Daniel

I felt better.

Anger and compassion, what strange twins.

The next morning, I drove to the institution, filled out and signed a truckful of forms, and left with the state supplied box of my wife's ashes.

I decided to celebrate her funeral at the sacred hill above Lake Shasta. Local tribes believe it is the center of creation, and I thought Charlene would feel at home there.

On the upper slopes of the mountain, they tell live stories of ghostly dwarves in green robes who manage the life-growth of the trees, spirits of good will who inhabit the stone stomach of the great peaks.

I drove as far up as the road would go and got out of the car to smell the crisp air and to feel the uncanny warmth of the high sun. I walked higher to a clearing with a great stone situated near a lone sycamore, a place known to a few, where the bright granite outcropping of earth's creative center leans out and up toward the unending and ever-expanding fruit of the universe.

I did not throw her ashes or disperse them in any way. Instead, I dug a hole beneath the boulder, close to its powerful spirit. I placed the box in the hole and covered it so that Charlene could rest a while before she journeyed further into the beyond.

I looked down upon the water below accentuated by hillsides of dark green forests. The surface shimmered as a soft wind blew.

As I prayed, I took my letter to her and tore it to tiny pieces, like a shredded secret message, and I released it into the heart of the wind, free to seek its own place of rest too.

On the way home, I bought a French café table and two chairs. I put them on the deck.

Now, on weekend mornings, I make coffee and pour two cups, one for Charlene and one for me.

My life has not been perfect since her death, but the love we share sustains me, and through it, I learned that forgiveness can heal harsh circumstances, like the unfair wrongs that friends sometimes inflict, or the unfair illnesses of human contamination.

Like Mark's ghost, Charlene's spirit sometimes visits. Once, while frying chicken in lard, the phone rang. Mr. Ronni, working the weekend, wanted an explanation about some cost figures, and our discussion extended awhile. Suddenly, the phone went dead. I called him back but received a dial tone. Just as suddenly, I smelled smoke and remembered the chicken. The grease had gotten so hot, it burst to flames. I covered the pan, and fortunately, there was no real damage, except to the chicken.

Charlene did that. Protected me.

It is late, time for sleep. As I look forward to my continuing days, I am comforted knowing that the Lord prepared Charlene's very own mansion in heaven, and she resides there now, without her demons, without drugs, and without those annoying tardive dyskinesia twitches. I know

He designed it to accommodate her and her adventurous imagination.

I bet there are hummingbirds, too.

Made in the USA
Las Vegas, NV
04 May 2022